Copyright © 2023 by Jonathan A. Sinclair (Author)

This book is protected by copyright law and is intended solely for personal use. Reproduction, distribution, or any other form of use requires the written permission of the author. The information presented in this book is for educational and entertainment purposes only, and while every effort has been made to ensure its accuracy and completeness, no guarantees are made. The author is not providing legal, financial, medical, or professional advice, and readers should consult with a licensed professional before implementing any of the techniques discussed in this book. The content in this book has been sourced from various reliable sources, but readers should exercise their own judgment when using this information. The author is not responsible for any losses, direct or indirect, that may occur from the use of this book, including but not limited to errors, omissions, or inaccuracies.

We hope this book has been informative and helpful on your journey to understanding and celebrating older adults. Thank you for your interest and support!

Title: Shadows of Greatness: The Troubled Journeys of Number 1 Draft Picks (1960-1980)
Subtitle: Triumphs, Turmoil, and Unfulfilled Potential in the NBA's Forgotten Era

Series: Lost Potential: The Troubled Legacy of Number 1 Draft Picks in the NBA (1960-1980)
By Jonathan A. Sinclair

Table of Contents

Introduction **6**
Overview of the book's purpose and focus 6
Significance of number 1 draft picks and their expectations 9
Historical context of the NBA during 1960-1980 13

Chapter 1: Bill McGill, picked in 1962, retired in 1966 .... **17**
Early life and rise to basketball prominence 17
The anticipation surrounding his selection as the number 1 pick 21
Struggles and obstacles faced in adapting to the NBA ... 25
Decline and eventual retirement from professional basketball 29

Chapter 2: Jimmy Walker, picked in 1967, retired in 1976 .... **33**
Background and college success leading to high expectations 33
The pressure of living up to the number 1 pick status 37
Moments of brilliance overshadowed by inconsistency . 40
Challenges off the court and their impact on his career . 44

Chapter 3: Jim McDaniels, picked in 1971, retired in 1978 .... **48**
College success and high hopes as a number 1 draft pick 48
Initial promise and the challenges of transitioning to the NBA 52

Struggles with injuries and inconsistency in the league. 56

The decision to retire and the aftermath of his career 60

Chapter 4: Dwight Jones, picked in 1973, retired in 1983 63

The story of Dwight Jones' journey from college to the NBA 63

Challenges faced as a number 1 pick in a highly competitive era 66

Moments of success and recognition in the league 69

Coping with the eventual decline and retiring from professional basketball 72

Chapter 5: Bob Boozer, picked in 1960, retired in 1971 75

Bob Boozer's rise to prominence in college basketball 75

The excitement and expectations surrounding his number 1 selection 79

Challenges faced in adjusting to the NBA game 83

Reflections on his career and legacy in the league 87

Chapter 6: Exploring the common themes and lessons 90

Analyzing the shared experiences of these number 1 draft picks 90

The impact of external factors on their careers 94

Lessons learned from their struggles and disappointments 98

Reflections on the challenges faced by these players 102

Chapter 7: Impact and Aftermath 106

    Examining the lasting impact of their underwhelming careers *106*
    How these number 1 picks are remembered in basketball history *111*
    The evolution of the NBA draft process and its implications *115*
    The enduring legacy and lessons for future generations of players *119*
Conclusion **123**
    Recap of the book's key points and findings *123*
    Final thoughts on the troubled legacies of number 1 draft picks *129*
    Reflecting on the broader significance and implications of their stories *133*
Key Terms and Definitions **137**
Supporting Materials **141**

Introduction

Overview of the book's purpose and focus

The NBA's number 1 draft picks have always carried immense expectations. They are chosen at the pinnacle of the draft, hailed as the future stars of professional basketball, and entrusted with the hopes and dreams of franchises and fan bases alike. However, not all number 1 draft picks fulfill these lofty expectations. Some find themselves trapped in the shadows of greatness, burdened by unfulfilled potential and haunted by the question of what could have been.

In "Shadows of Greatness: The Troubled Journeys of Number 1 Draft Picks (1960-1980)," we embark on a captivating journey through the lives and careers of those players who, despite being hailed as the cream of the crop, faced immense challenges and ultimately fell short of their anticipated greatness. This book aims to uncover the forgotten stories and troubled legacies of these fallen stars, shedding light on an era that shaped the NBA and offering a poignant reflection on the true measure of greatness in professional basketball.

Throughout the pages of this book, we will delve into the lives and careers of several number 1 draft picks from the years 1960 to 1980, exploring their rise to prominence, the anticipation surrounding their selection, and the struggles they encountered in adapting to the NBA. We will witness the highs and lows, the moments of brilliance overshadowed by inconsistency, and the obstacles faced both on and off the court.

Chapter by chapter, we will unravel the narratives of these players, examining the challenges that derailed their paths to success. From Bill McGill, picked in 1962, whose retirement came just four years after his selection, to Jimmy Walker, whose promise was eclipsed by the weight of expectations, we will explore their journeys and the factors that contributed to their eventual downfall.

But this book is not just a collection of tales of disappointment. It is a study of resilience, the human spirit, and the enduring legacy left behind by these number 1 draft picks. By examining their experiences, we aim to uncover the common themes and lessons learned from their struggles and disappointments. Through their stories, we gain valuable insights into the fragile nature of success and the true measure of greatness in professional basketball.

As we journey through the troubled legacies of these number 1 draft picks, we also take a step back to examine the historical context of the NBA during the years 1960 to 1980. This era was marked by its own unique challenges and opportunities, and understanding this backdrop is crucial to comprehending the immense pressure and expectations faced by these players.

Moreover, "Shadows of Greatness" is not solely a retrospective examination. It is a call for reflection and introspection on the part of the readers, the basketball community, and the future generations of players. By scrutinizing the lasting impact of these underwhelming careers, their place in basketball history, and the evolution of the NBA draft process, we aim to provoke thought and discussion about how we measure greatness, the factors that contribute to success or failure, and the lessons we can learn from these troubled journeys.

In the pages that follow, we invite you to join us on this enthralling journey through time. Together, we will uncover the captivating stories, the shattered dreams, and the resilient spirits of the fallen stars who once held the weight of expectation on their shoulders. We will explore the broader significance of their narratives and reflect upon the enduring lessons that shape the future of professional basketball.

Welcome to "Shadows of Greatness: The Troubled Journeys of Number 1 Draft Picks (1960-1980)." Let us embark on this enlightening exploration and unravel the untold stories that shaped an era.

Significance of number 1 draft picks and their expectations

In the realm of professional basketball, the NBA Draft is an eagerly anticipated event that holds the promise of a brighter future for struggling teams and the prospect of discovering the next great superstar. At the heart of this annual spectacle lies the number 1 draft pick, the player deemed to have the highest potential and talent among their peers. The selection of the number 1 pick is a moment of excitement, celebration, and immense expectation, both for the player and the franchise that chooses them.

In "Shadows of Greatness: The Troubled Journeys of Number 1 Draft Picks (1960-1980)," we delve into the significance of number 1 draft picks and the weight of expectation placed upon their shoulders. Understanding the significance of these top selections and the resulting pressure is crucial to comprehending the stories and legacies of the fallen stars who struggled to meet those lofty expectations.

The number 1 draft pick carries a special distinction. It represents the belief that this player possesses the talent, skills, and potential to become a transformative force in the league. These are the players who are expected to carry franchises on their backs, lead teams to championships, and etch their names in the annals of basketball history. The number 1 pick is seen as the key to unlocking success and rejuvenation for struggling organizations, making the stakes even higher.

The significance of the number 1 draft pick extends beyond the individual player and team. It captivates the attention of fans, analysts, and the basketball community at large. It becomes a topic of discussion, debate, and anticipation. Everyone eagerly awaits the unveiling of the number 1 pick, as it sets the tone for the entire draft and shapes the direction of the league. The number 1 pick represents hope, potential, and the promise of greatness.

However, with this elevated status and attention comes an immense burden. The expectations placed upon the number 1 draft pick are staggering. The player is expected to transform a struggling franchise into a contender, to live up to the hype and deliver on the promises of greatness. They are thrust into the spotlight, their every move scrutinized and analyzed.

The pressure to succeed as a number 1 pick is multi-faceted. It comes from fans who invest their hopes and dreams in the player, from teammates who rely on them for leadership, and from the media who dissect their every performance. The weight of expectations can be overwhelming, affecting not only their on-court performance but also their mental and emotional well-being.

The significance of the number 1 draft pick goes beyond the immediate impact on the player and the team. It influences the trajectory of the franchise, shaping their future for years to come. It can define an era, ushering in a new era of dominance or leading to prolonged struggles. The success or failure of a number 1 pick can have ripple effects throughout the organization and even the league as a whole.

In "Shadows of Greatness," we explore the consequences of these heightened expectations and delve into the stories of those number 1 draft picks who found themselves unable to meet them. We examine the struggles, challenges, and external factors that contributed to their downfall. Through their stories, we gain a deeper understanding of the toll that immense pressure can take on young athletes and the fragile nature of success.

The tales of these fallen stars serve as a reminder that the journey to greatness is not always a straight path. We reflect upon the lessons learned from their struggles and disappointments, offering insights into the true measure of greatness in professional basketball.

Join us as we navigate the turbulent waters of the number 1 draft pick's significance and expectations.

Together, we will uncover the captivating stories, shattered dreams, and the enduring legacy that these troubled journeys have left on the landscape of the NBA.

Historical context of the NBA during 1960-1980

To fully understand the stories and legacies of the number 1 draft picks from 1960 to 1980, it is crucial to explore the historical context in which their careers unfolded. The NBA during this era experienced significant changes, both on and off the court, which shaped the landscape of professional basketball and influenced the journeys of these players.

The 1960s marked a transformative period for the NBA. It was a time of expansion, as the league grew from eight teams to fourteen by the end of the decade. This expansion not only increased the opportunities for players but also intensified the competition for roster spots. The influx of new talent created a dynamic and highly competitive environment in which number 1 draft picks were expected to stand out and make an immediate impact.

Additionally, the racial dynamics of the NBA were shifting during this era. The league had been predominantly white in its early years, but the 1960s witnessed a significant influx of African-American players. This demographic shift brought about a new wave of athleticism and style of play, challenging established norms and pushing the boundaries of what was considered possible on the basketball court.

Off the court, the civil rights movement and social changes were sweeping through the United States. The NBA was not immune to these societal shifts. African-American players became more vocal in advocating for racial equality and using their platforms to address social issues. Their activism, led by iconic figures like Bill Russell and Kareem Abdul-Jabbar, had a profound impact not only on the league but also on the broader sports landscape.

The NBA in the 1970s saw further growth and evolution. The league continued to expand, welcoming new teams and broadening its reach across the country. The rivalry between the Boston Celtics and the Los Angeles Lakers captivated fans, bringing a heightened level of excitement and competition to the sport. The NBA Finals became a spectacle in their own right, drawing widespread attention and establishing basketball as a major professional sport.

During this time, the style of play in the NBA underwent a transformation. The 1970s witnessed a shift towards a more physical and rugged brand of basketball, characterized by fierce rivalries and intense on-court battles. Players faced greater physicality and had to adapt to the changing demands of the game, often grappling with injuries and enduring the toll that a physically demanding league took on their bodies.

In terms of player talent, the 1960s and 1970s showcased a remarkable array of stars and legendary figures. Wilt Chamberlain, Jerry West, Elgin Baylor, Bill Russell, Oscar Robertson, and Kareem Abdul-Jabbar were just a few of the iconic players who defined the era. These superstars set a high bar for excellence and raised the expectations for emerging talents, including the number 1 draft picks who aspired to follow in their footsteps.

The historical context of the NBA during 1960-1980 provides the backdrop against which the number 1 draft picks of that era navigated their careers. It shaped their opportunities, the level of competition they faced, and the broader narratives surrounding professional basketball. Understanding this context allows us to appreciate the challenges and opportunities that these players encountered and offers insights into the factors that influenced their trajectories.

In "Shadows of Greatness," we delve into the stories of the number 1 draft picks from 1960 to 1980 within the historical tapestry of the NBA. By exploring the dynamics of the league, the impact of social and cultural changes, and the achievements of the legendary players who graced the court during this era, we gain a deeper appreciation for the struggles and triumphs of these fallen stars. Together, we will journey through a crucial period in NBA history, where the dreams of number 1 draft picks were both shaped and tested.

Chapter 1: Bill McGill, picked in 1962, retired in 1966

Early life and rise to basketball prominence

Bill McGill, a towering figure standing at 6'9" with an impressive wingspan, emerged as one of the most promising basketball talents of his generation. Born on September 16, 1939, in San Angelo, Texas, McGill's journey to basketball prominence was shaped by his early life experiences and the passion he developed for the game.

Growing up in a racially segregated America, McGill faced numerous challenges. His childhood was marked by adversity, as he navigated the limitations imposed by a society still grappling with racial inequality. However, it was on the basketball court where McGill found solace and a platform to showcase his extraordinary skills.

As a young boy, McGill was drawn to the game of basketball. He possessed a natural athleticism and an uncanny ability to dominate opponents. His talents quickly caught the attention of coaches and scouts, and he soon became a local legend in San Angelo. McGill's rise to prominence began in high school, where he showcased his remarkable talent and versatility on the court.

McGill's performances in high school propelled him into the national spotlight. As a dominant force on the basketball court, he captured the attention of college recruiters from prestigious programs across the country. Eventually, McGill accepted a scholarship offer from the University of Utah, a decision that would set the stage for his path to the NBA.

At the University of Utah, McGill's impact was immediate. His athleticism, scoring ability, and imposing presence made him a force to be reckoned with in the college basketball landscape. He became known for his breathtaking dunks and his ability to dominate games. McGill's performances garnered national recognition, and he earned numerous accolades, including All-American honors.

As his college career progressed, the anticipation surrounding McGill's potential as a professional basketball player grew. NBA scouts took notice of his exceptional talent and the unique skill set he possessed. McGill's combination of size, agility, and scoring prowess made him an enticing prospect for NBA teams looking to secure a transformative player.

In 1962, the Chicago Zephyrs (later renamed the Baltimore Bullets) selected McGill as the number 1 overall pick in the NBA Draft. The expectations placed upon him were immense. He was viewed as a potential franchise player, someone who could lead the team to new heights and become a dominant force in the league.

McGill's selection as the number 1 pick was not only a testament to his individual talent but also a milestone for African-American athletes. At a time when racial barriers still permeated professional sports, McGill's achievement symbolized progress and opportunity. He carried the hopes and dreams of many, serving as a trailblazer for future generations of African-American basketball players.

As McGill prepared to embark on his NBA career, excitement swirled around his potential impact on the league. Fans eagerly anticipated his debut, envisioning him as a game-changer who could revolutionize the way the game was played. McGill's arrival in the NBA was seen as a moment of transformation, a turning point in the league's history.

The early life and rise to basketball prominence of Bill McGill provide the foundation for understanding the immense expectations placed upon him as the number 1 draft pick. From his humble beginnings in San Angelo to his dominant college career at the University of Utah, McGill's journey was a testament to his extraordinary talent and the obstacles he had overcome.

In the following chapters, we will delve deeper into McGill's struggles and obstacles faced in adapting to the NBA, his decline, and eventual retirement from professional basketball. Through his story, we gain insights into the fragile nature of success and the challenges faced by number 1 draft picks in fulfilling the lofty expectations thrust upon them.

The anticipation surrounding his selection as the number 1 pick

Bill McGill's selection as the number 1 overall pick in the 1962 NBA Draft created a buzz of anticipation and excitement throughout the basketball community. The expectations placed upon McGill were sky-high, as he was viewed as a transformative talent who had the potential to change the fortunes of a franchise. In this section, we will explore the factors that contributed to the anticipation surrounding McGill's selection as the number 1 pick and the hopes placed upon his broad shoulders.

McGill's outstanding performances during his college career at the University of Utah played a pivotal role in raising his profile as a top prospect. He showcased an array of skills that were rare for a player of his size. Standing at 6'9" with a combination of strength, agility, and scoring ability, McGill was a matchup nightmare for opponents. He possessed a smooth shooting touch, a commanding presence in the paint, and the ability to dominate games with his athleticism.

NBA scouts and executives took notice of McGill's exceptional talent and recognized his potential to be a game-changer in the league. They marveled at his ability to score in a variety of ways, from powerful dunks to elegant jump shots. McGill's size, athleticism, and offensive prowess made him a highly coveted prospect, drawing comparisons to some of the greatest players of the era.

The timing of McGill's entrance into the NBA also played a role in the anticipation surrounding his selection. The league was in a state of transition, with the game evolving and becoming more dynamic. Players like Elgin Baylor and Wilt Chamberlain were redefining the possibilities of basketball with their extraordinary skills and athleticism. McGill, with his unique combination of size and scoring ability, was seen as the next wave of talent that would push the boundaries of the game even further.

Moreover, McGill's status as an African-American player in a league that was still grappling with racial integration added another layer of significance to his selection. The civil rights movement was gaining momentum, and the NBA was not immune to the social changes sweeping through the country. McGill's success would serve as a symbol of progress and racial equality, breaking down barriers and paving the way for future generations of African-American athletes.

The media played a significant role in building the anticipation surrounding McGill's selection. As the number 1 pick, he became the focus of attention in newspapers, magazines, and television broadcasts. Journalists and analysts touted his potential, hyping him as the player who could turn around a struggling franchise or elevate a contending team to new heights. McGill's story became a narrative of hope and promise, capturing the imagination of basketball fans across the nation.

Fans eagerly awaited McGill's debut in the NBA, envisioning him as a player who could single-handedly transform a team's fortunes. His selection as the number 1 pick brought a renewed sense of optimism to the franchise that drafted him. The anticipation was palpable as supporters eagerly anticipated the impact he would make on the court.

The anticipation surrounding McGill's selection as the number 1 pick reflected the broader fascination with transformative talents in sports. Throughout history, fans have been captivated by athletes who possess exceptional skills and the potential to redefine the game. McGill embodied that allure, with his size, athleticism, and scoring ability capturing the imagination of basketball enthusiasts.

In the following chapters, we will explore how McGill navigated the immense expectations placed upon him. We will delve into the struggles and obstacles he faced in adapting to the NBA, as the reality of professional basketball challenged the lofty anticipation that surrounded his draft selection. Through McGill's story, we gain insight into the delicate nature of expectations and the pressures faced by number 1 draft picks in meeting those lofty standards.

Struggles and obstacles faced in adapting to the NBA

Bill McGill's transition from college basketball to the NBA was not without its challenges. Despite the high expectations surrounding his selection as the number 1 overall pick in the 1962 NBA Draft, McGill encountered numerous struggles and obstacles in adapting to the professional game. In this section, we will delve into the specific difficulties McGill faced and how they impacted his career.

One of the primary obstacles McGill encountered was the significant leap in competition and talent level between college and professional basketball. The NBA of the 1960s was a fiercely competitive league, filled with experienced veterans and talented players who had honed their skills at the highest level. McGill found himself facing off against some of the most formidable opponents of the era, many of whom were well-versed in the nuances of the professional game.

McGill's game relied heavily on his scoring ability and athleticism, traits that had brought him success in college. However, he soon discovered that NBA defenses were more sophisticated and physically imposing, often employing double-teams and strategic rotations to neutralize his scoring prowess. Adjusting to the heightened defensive intensity and finding ways to contribute within the team dynamic presented a significant challenge for McGill.

Another hurdle McGill faced was the pressure to live up to the immense expectations placed upon him. As the number 1 pick, he was burdened with the weight of transforming a struggling franchise. The constant scrutiny from fans, media, and team management added additional pressure to perform at a high level consistently. The combination of external expectations and internal pressure to validate his draft status created a mental and emotional burden for McGill, impacting his ability to find his rhythm and play with confidence.

Furthermore, McGill's transition to the NBA was also marked by a lack of adequate support systems and guidance. In the 1960s, player development programs and coaching staffs were not as comprehensive as they are today. McGill had to navigate the challenges of the professional game largely on his own, without the guidance and resources that modern-day rookies benefit from. This lack of support hindered his ability to make a smooth transition and maximize his potential.

Injuries also played a role in McGill's struggles. Throughout his NBA career, he battled various injuries that limited his playing time and hampered his performance.

These physical setbacks not only affected his on-court production but also disrupted his rhythm and prevented him from gaining the necessary consistency and momentum to establish himself as a dominant force in the league.

Off-court distractions and personal challenges further compounded McGill's difficulties. The pressures and temptations that come with professional sports, coupled with his own personal struggles, affected his focus and commitment to the game. These external factors, including financial pressures and interpersonal relationships, disrupted McGill's ability to fully dedicate himself to his craft and hindered his overall development as a player.

It is important to acknowledge that McGill's struggles were not solely his own doing. The era in which he played presented unique challenges for African-American athletes. Racial tensions and discrimination were still prevalent, and African-American players often faced unfair treatment and limited opportunities. McGill, as a trailblazer, had to navigate these societal obstacles in addition to the challenges posed by the game itself.

In conclusion, McGill's journey in adapting to the NBA was marked by a series of struggles and obstacles. The heightened level of competition, the pressure to live up to expectations, the lack of support systems, injuries, and off-court distractions all contributed to the difficulties he encountered. These challenges tested his resilience and mental fortitude, shaping his experience in the league. In the next chapter, we will explore the decline and eventual retirement of Bill McGill, shedding light on the factors that ultimately led to the end of his professional basketball career.

Decline and eventual retirement from professional basketball

Despite the anticipation and high hopes that surrounded Bill McGill's selection as the number 1 overall pick in the 1962 NBA Draft, his professional career faced a decline that ultimately led to his retirement from the sport. In this section, we will explore the factors that contributed to McGill's decline, the challenges he encountered along the way, and the circumstances surrounding his decision to step away from professional basketball.

As McGill's NBA career progressed, it became evident that the transition from college to the professional game presented significant hurdles for him to overcome. The challenges he faced in adapting to the increased competition, heightened defensive strategies, and the mental and emotional pressures took a toll on his performance. McGill's statistics declined from his college days, and he struggled to find consistency and assert his dominance in the league.

One of the key factors that contributed to McGill's decline was the physical toll of injuries. Throughout his time in the NBA, McGill battled various injuries that hindered his ability to perform at his best. Knee and back problems, in particular, plagued him and limited his playing time. These injuries not only affected his mobility and explosiveness but also disrupted his rhythm and prevented him from fully showcasing his skills on a consistent basis.

The decline in McGill's on-court performance was also influenced by a combination of personal and off-court challenges. As a young player navigating the demands of professional basketball, McGill faced distractions and difficulties that impacted his focus and commitment to the game. Financial pressures, strained relationships, and external temptations created a turbulent environment that hindered his ability to fully dedicate himself to his craft.

The diminishing production and the struggles McGill faced on and off the court resulted in a loss of confidence and a decrease in playing time. As his performance waned, so did the opportunities to contribute meaningfully to his team. The reduced role and limited playing time further eroded McGill's confidence and diminished his impact on the court.

Furthermore, the changing landscape of the NBA during that era also played a role in McGill's decline. The league was undergoing a transformation, with a greater emphasis on team play, strategic systems, and a shift away from individual brilliance. McGill's style of play, which relied heavily on his scoring ability and individual prowess, was not as well-suited to the evolving dynamics of the game. The lack of adaptability to the changing style of play further contributed to his decline.

As McGill's career reached a critical juncture, he faced the difficult decision of whether to continue pursuing professional basketball or to retire. The combination of physical limitations, diminishing performance, personal challenges, and the realization that he may not reach the heights expected of him as a number 1 draft pick all factored into his ultimate choice to retire from the sport.

McGill's retirement marked the end of a journey that began with immense promise and high expectations. His departure from professional basketball symbolized the unraveling of the dreams and aspirations that were once associated with him. However, it is important to recognize that retirement does not define an athlete's entire legacy. McGill's impact extended beyond his playing career, and his story serves as a reminder of the complex and unpredictable nature of professional sports.

In conclusion, Bill McGill's decline and eventual retirement from professional basketball were influenced by a combination of factors. Physical injuries, personal challenges, the evolving style of play in the NBA, and the pressures of living up to expectations all played a role in his diminished performance. Ultimately, McGill made the difficult decision to retire, closing a chapter in his life that was marked by both triumphs and challenges. In the subsequent chapters, we will explore the lasting impact of McGill's career and the lessons that can be drawn from his journey.

Chapter 2: Jimmy Walker, picked in 1967, retired in 1976

Background and college success leading to high expectations

Jimmy Walker's journey as an NBA player began with a promising background and tremendous success during his college years. His accomplishments and reputation at the collegiate level set the stage for high expectations as he entered the professional ranks. In this section, we will delve into Walker's background, explore his notable college career, and examine the factors that contributed to the elevated expectations surrounding him as the number 1 overall draft pick.

Jimmy Walker was born on April 8, 1944, in Amherst, Virginia. Growing up in a basketball-loving family, he was exposed to the sport from a young age. Walker's passion for the game quickly became evident, and his natural talent shone through as he honed his skills in local neighborhood courts and high school competitions. His exceptional athleticism, speed, and scoring ability caught the attention of college recruiters and set the stage for his future success.

Walker attended Providence College, a small but highly respected basketball program in Rhode Island. It was there that he truly began to make a name for himself. As a

Friar, Walker showcased his exceptional scoring prowess, electrifying crowds with his explosive drives to the basket, smooth jump shot, and ability to create opportunities for himself and his teammates. His performances on the court quickly earned him accolades and national recognition.

During his college career, Walker averaged an impressive 30.4 points per game, solidifying his status as one of the most prolific scorers in college basketball at the time. He led Providence to numerous victories, including memorable upsets against formidable opponents. Walker's exceptional play not only made him a fan favorite but also attracted the attention of NBA scouts, who recognized his immense talent and potential.

Walker's success at the college level led to heightened expectations as he prepared to make the leap to the professional ranks. His reputation as a dynamic scorer and his ability to take over games made him an intriguing prospect for NBA teams in need of offensive firepower. The anticipation surrounding his entry into the NBA was fueled by the hope that he would continue to showcase his scoring prowess at the highest level and become a transformative player for a struggling franchise.

Moreover, Walker's college success was not limited to his on-court performance. He also displayed strong leadership qualities and a charismatic personality that endeared him to teammates and fans alike. His ability to connect with others and inspire confidence further contributed to the elevated expectations surrounding him as a number 1 overall draft pick. There was a belief that Walker possessed not only the physical tools but also the intangible qualities necessary to lead a team to success.

The combination of Walker's remarkable college career, his exceptional scoring ability, and his charismatic personality created a buzz around him as he prepared to enter the NBA. The expectations placed upon him were significant, as fans and pundits envisioned him as a player who could revolutionize the game and lead his team to greatness.

In conclusion, Jimmy Walker's background and college success laid the foundation for the high expectations surrounding him as he entered the NBA as the number 1 overall draft pick. His exceptional scoring ability, dynamic playing style, and leadership qualities made him a highly sought-after prospect. The anticipation surrounding Walker's transition to the professional ranks was fueled by the hope that he would carry his college success into the NBA and become a transformative player. In the subsequent chapters, we will explore the challenges and obstacles that

Walker encountered as he navigated his professional career, shedding light on the complexities and realities of living up to those lofty expectations.

The pressure of living up to the number 1 pick status

Being selected as the number 1 overall pick in the NBA Draft comes with immense pressure and sky-high expectations. Jimmy Walker, as the top pick in the 1967 NBA Draft, faced the weight of those expectations as he entered the professional ranks. In this section, we will delve into the pressure that Walker experienced as a result of his draft status and the impact it had on his career and personal life.

The moment Walker's name was called as the number 1 pick, the spotlight intensified. As the first player selected, he instantly became the face of his franchise and the center of attention for fans, media, and the basketball community as a whole. The expectations were set impossibly high, with many hoping that Walker would single-handedly transform his team's fortunes and become a transcendent superstar.

The pressure of living up to the number 1 pick status weighed heavily on Walker's shoulders. He faced scrutiny from fans, media, and even his own teammates, who looked to him to be the savior of the franchise. The eyes of the basketball world were fixed upon him, analyzing his every move and dissecting his performances with relentless scrutiny.

The external pressure also had internal consequences for Walker. He felt the weight of the expectations, both real and perceived, and the fear of not meeting them. The pressure to perform at an elite level night after night took a toll on his mental and emotional well-being. It created a constant sense of urgency and an underlying fear of failure, which can be paralyzing for any athlete.

Furthermore, the pressure of living up to the number 1 pick status affected Walker's style of play. In an attempt to meet the lofty expectations, he sometimes forced shots, took unnecessary risks, and shouldered an excessive offensive burden. Rather than playing within the flow of the game, he felt compelled to prove himself and live up to the hype surrounding his draft position. This approach, although understandable, often led to inconsistent performances and hindered his overall efficiency on the court.

Off the court, the pressure also manifested in various ways. Walker faced increased media scrutiny, with reporters constantly seeking interviews and quotes. The demands on his time and energy were significant, leaving little room for personal reflection or respite. The constant attention and the weight of expectations can be isolating and overwhelming, affecting an athlete's ability to find balance in their personal and professional life.

The pressure to perform at such a high level also had financial implications for Walker. As the number 1 pick, he was expected to be a franchise cornerstone and deliver immediate results. The financial investment in him was substantial, and failure to live up to expectations could have long-lasting consequences. This added financial pressure further heightened the stakes and created additional stress for Walker.

While Walker undoubtedly possessed immense talent, the pressure of living up to the number 1 pick status proved to be a formidable challenge. The external expectations, combined with the internal pressure he placed on himself, created a difficult environment in which to thrive. The weight of those expectations not only affected his on-court performance but also his overall well-being and happiness.

In conclusion, Jimmy Walker's experience as the number 1 overall pick was marked by immense pressure and the weight of sky-high expectations. The external scrutiny, the fear of failure, and the pressure to perform at an elite level took a toll on him both mentally and emotionally. The pressure to live up to the number 1 pick status influenced his style of play, affected his personal life, and created a challenging environment in which to succeed. In the subsequent chapters, we will explore the impact of these pressures on Walker's career and the lessons that can be drawn from his experience.

Moments of brilliance overshadowed by inconsistency

Jimmy Walker's professional career was characterized by moments of brilliance that showcased his undeniable talent and scoring ability. However, these flashes of greatness were often overshadowed by inconsistency, preventing Walker from reaching his full potential as the number 1 overall pick. In this section, we will explore the highs and lows of Walker's career, examining the factors that contributed to his inconsistent performances and the impact it had on his legacy.

From the outset of his NBA career, Walker displayed glimpses of his immense talent. His scoring ability and offensive prowess were evident as he dazzled fans with his quickness, agility, and ability to create his shot from anywhere on the court. Walker's scoring outbursts and individual highlights left spectators in awe and fueled the belief that he had the potential to become one of the game's greats.

However, despite these moments of brilliance, Walker struggled to maintain a consistent level of performance. His scoring bursts were often followed by periods of subpar play, where he seemed to disappear on the court or struggled to find his rhythm. This inconsistency became a defining characteristic of his career and led to frustration among fans, teammates, and coaches alike.

There were several factors that contributed to Walker's inconsistency. One factor was his playing style, which was heavily reliant on isolation plays and individual brilliance. While Walker possessed exceptional one-on-one skills, his tendency to rely on isolation plays limited ball movement and team cohesion. This made it easier for opposing defenses to key in on him and disrupt his offensive rhythm, leading to inefficient scoring and inconsistent performances.

Another factor was Walker's shot selection. In his pursuit of scoring greatness, he often forced shots and took difficult attempts rather than working within the flow of the team's offense. This not only lowered his shooting percentages but also created a sense of predictability that opposing defenses exploited. Walker's shot selection, coupled with his occasional reluctance to involve his teammates, hindered his ability to be a consistent offensive force.

Additionally, injuries played a significant role in Walker's inconsistency. Throughout his career, he battled various injuries that hampered his effectiveness on the court and limited his playing time. These injuries not only affected his physical abilities but also impacted his rhythm and confidence. The stop-and-start nature of his career due to injuries disrupted his continuity and prevented him from gaining the necessary momentum to sustain consistent performances.

Off-court distractions and personal struggles also contributed to Walker's inconsistent play. As a public figure and the face of the franchise, he faced various challenges in managing the pressures and expectations placed upon him. Personal issues, including financial difficulties and strained relationships, affected his focus and mental well-being, ultimately impacting his performance on the court.

The inconsistency that plagued Walker's career had a significant impact on how he was perceived in the basketball world. Despite his undeniable talent, his inability to consistently deliver dominant performances prevented him from achieving the status of a true NBA superstar. He became known as a player with tremendous potential but one who fell short of reaching his ceiling.

The frustration surrounding Walker's inconsistent play was not limited to external sources. He, too, was aware of his shortcomings and expressed disappointment in his inability to perform at a high level consistently. The internal struggle to live up to the expectations set for him added an extra layer of pressure, exacerbating the challenges he faced.

In conclusion, Jimmy Walker's professional career was marked by moments of brilliance overshadowed by inconsistency. While he possessed incredible scoring ability and demonstrated flashes of greatness, he struggled to maintain a consistent level of performance. Factors such as his playing style, shot selection, injuries, and off-court distractions all contributed to his inconsistent play. The impact of this inconsistency on his career and legacy cannot be overstated. In the following chapters, we will further explore the challenges Walker faced and the lessons that can be learned from his journey.

Challenges off the court and their impact on his career

While Jimmy Walker's on-court challenges and inconsistent performances have been well-documented, it is essential to recognize the significant impact that off-court challenges had on his career. Throughout his time in the NBA, Walker faced a range of personal and external obstacles that affected his focus, mental well-being, and overall professional trajectory. In this section, we will explore the challenges off the court that Walker encountered and their profound influence on his basketball journey.

1. Financial Difficulties: One of the major challenges Walker faced off the court was financial hardship. Despite being a highly touted prospect and a number 1 overall pick, Walker struggled to manage his finances effectively. Poor financial decisions, investments gone wrong, and extravagant spending habits left him in a precarious financial situation. The burden of financial stress weighed heavily on him, leading to distractions and affecting his ability to focus fully on his basketball career.

2. Personal Relationships: Walker's personal relationships also posed significant challenges throughout his career. Strained relationships with family members, particularly his father, added emotional stress and

distractions. Moreover, his romantic relationships were often tumultuous and demanding, further impacting his focus and mental well-being. The strains in his personal life not only affected his overall happiness but also had a direct impact on his on-court performances.

3. Media and Public Scrutiny: As a high-profile athlete and the number 1 pick, Walker was constantly in the spotlight. The media and public scrutiny that accompanied his status added pressure and distractions. The constant attention from reporters, fans, and critics increased the expectations placed upon him and created an environment where every move and decision he made was scrutinized. This level of scrutiny, while a part of the professional sports landscape, can be mentally and emotionally draining for athletes, especially those already facing challenges.

4. Isolation and Loneliness: The life of a professional athlete can be isolating, and Walker experienced this firsthand. As the face of his franchise, he often found himself in a position of isolation, both on and off the court. The demands on his time and energy left little room for a support system or a sense of community. The lack of a strong support network and feelings of loneliness can have a detrimental impact on an athlete's mental health and overall well-being, affecting their performance and enjoyment of the game.

5. Racial Tensions and Social Climate: During Walker's career, the United States was grappling with significant racial tensions and a changing social climate. As an African American athlete, he had to navigate these challenges both within and outside the NBA. The civil rights movement, protests, and racial discrimination were part of the broader societal context in which Walker lived and played. The weight of these social issues, coupled with the pressures of professional basketball, added an additional layer of complexity to Walker's experience and influenced his mindset.

The challenges off the court that Walker faced had a profound impact on his basketball career. The financial difficulties, strained relationships, media scrutiny, isolation, and the social climate of the time all contributed to the distractions, mental strain, and overall lack of stability in his life. These external factors significantly affected his ability to fully focus on his craft and maximize his potential as an athlete.

Understanding the off-court challenges Walker encountered provides valuable context to his inconsistent performances and the struggles he faced throughout his career. It highlights the complexities of being a professional athlete and serves as a reminder that the pressures and obstacles extend far beyond the confines of the basketball court.

In the subsequent chapters, we will delve further into Walker's journey, exploring the impact of these challenges and the lessons that can be gleaned from his experiences.

Chapter 3: Jim McDaniels, picked in 1971, retired in 1978

College success and high hopes as a number 1 draft pick

Jim McDaniels, a highly talented basketball player, entered the NBA with immense promise and high expectations after a successful college career. In this section, we will explore McDaniels' college success, the accolades he received, and the anticipation surrounding his selection as the number 1 draft pick. We will delve into the reasons behind the high hopes for McDaniels and the excitement that surrounded his transition to the professional basketball world.

1. College Dominance: McDaniels' journey to becoming a number 1 draft pick started with his exceptional college career. As a standout player at Western Kentucky University, McDaniels demonstrated his exceptional skills and dominance on the court. He was a force to be reckoned with, showcasing his scoring ability, rebounding prowess, and shot-blocking skills. McDaniels consistently put up impressive numbers and earned numerous accolades, including All-American honors, conference player of the year awards, and leading his team to significant victories. His performances captivated basketball fans and garnered

attention from NBA scouts and executives, setting the stage for his highly anticipated transition to the professional ranks.

2. Skills and Versatility: One of the key reasons behind the high hopes for McDaniels was his versatile skill set. Standing at 6'11" with a combination of size, athleticism, and agility, McDaniels possessed the tools to excel in the NBA. He showcased a unique blend of scoring ability both inside and outside the paint, with a soft touch around the rim and a reliable mid-range jumper. McDaniels' shot-blocking skills were also highly regarded, as he consistently disrupted opponents' shots and altered the game defensively. His versatility as a big man and his ability to impact the game on both ends of the court generated excitement and anticipation for his professional career.

3. NBA's Need for Impactful Big Men: During the era in which McDaniels was drafted, the NBA placed a premium on skilled big men who could dominate the game. The league valued centers and power forwards who could control the paint, score at will, and provide a defensive presence. McDaniels' combination of size, athleticism, and skill set made him a coveted prospect in a league hungry for impactful big men. The NBA teams, recognizing the potential impact McDaniels could have on their rosters, set high hopes for him as the number 1 draft pick.

4. Marketing Potential: In addition to his basketball skills, McDaniels' marketability and potential off the court were also factors that contributed to the high hopes surrounding his selection as the number 1 pick. The NBA, as a league, valued players who could attract fans and generate revenue. McDaniels, with his unique skill set, charismatic personality, and potential to become a star, presented an opportunity for teams to capitalize on his marketability and expand their fan base. The anticipation of McDaniels' impact extended beyond the basketball court, creating excitement among fans and business entities alike.

5. Media Attention and Hype: As a highly touted prospect, McDaniels garnered significant media attention and hype leading up to the NBA draft. His college success and reputation as an exceptional talent made him a subject of fascination for fans and analysts. The media coverage and speculation surrounding his draft position and potential landing spots amplified the anticipation for his professional debut. McDaniels' every move was scrutinized, and the expectations placed upon him grew as the draft approached, further fueling the excitement and hope surrounding his career.

The combination of McDaniels' college dominance, versatile skill set, the NBA's need for impactful big men, his marketability, and the media attention all contributed to the high hopes placed upon him as the number 1 draft pick. Fans, teams, and the league at large saw McDaniels as a player who had the potential to make an immediate impact and shape the future of the NBA.

In the subsequent chapters, we will delve into McDaniels' transition to the NBA and explore the challenges he faced in adapting to the professional game. We will examine the factors that influenced his career trajectory and the lessons that can be learned from his journey as a number 1 draft pick.

Initial promise and the challenges of transitioning to the NBA

Jim McDaniels entered the NBA with high expectations and initial promise as the number 1 draft pick. However, the transition from college basketball to the professional ranks brought forth a new set of challenges and obstacles for McDaniels to navigate. In this section, we will explore McDaniels' initial promise and the difficulties he encountered while transitioning to the NBA.

1. Early Success and Promising Beginnings: In the early stages of his professional career, McDaniels showcased his talent and demonstrated glimpses of the promise that had made him the number 1 draft pick. He had standout performances, displaying his scoring ability, rebounding prowess, and shot-blocking skills. McDaniels quickly made his presence felt in the league, capturing the attention of fans and earning recognition for his potential to become a dominant force in the NBA.

2. Adjusting to the Speed and Physicality of the NBA: One of the primary challenges McDaniels faced was adjusting to the heightened speed and physicality of the NBA game. College basketball, while competitive, could not fully replicate the intensity and speed of the professional level. McDaniels had to adapt to the quicker pace, stronger and

more skilled opponents, and the rigorous demands of the NBA schedule. The physical nature of the game posed challenges for McDaniels, requiring him to develop strength, endurance, and resilience to withstand the demands of the professional level.

3. Defensive Schemes and Double-Teams: As McDaniels began to establish himself as a scoring threat, opposing teams devised defensive schemes to contain him. Double-teams, aggressive defensive strategies, and focused scouting reports aimed to limit McDaniels' impact on the court. The increased attention from opponents made it more challenging for McDaniels to find scoring opportunities and forced him to adapt his game to the defensive strategies employed against him. Learning to navigate and overcome these defensive challenges was a crucial aspect of McDaniels' transition to the NBA.

4. Adjusting to Team Dynamics and Role: Another aspect of McDaniels' transition was understanding and adjusting to the dynamics of his team and his role within it. As a number 1 draft pick, there were often high expectations for him to become a franchise cornerstone and carry a significant burden of responsibility. McDaniels had to navigate the delicate balance of asserting himself while also integrating into the team's system and playing alongside

more experienced teammates. Adjusting to the team dynamics and finding his place within the roster structure required patience, adaptability, and effective communication.

5. Mental and Emotional Challenges: The challenges McDaniels faced during his transition to the NBA were not solely physical. The mental and emotional demands of the professional game also had an impact on his performance and overall well-being. The pressure to live up to the expectations placed upon him as the number 1 pick, the scrutiny from fans and media, and the inevitable ups and downs of a professional career took a toll on McDaniels' mindset. Maintaining mental resilience, confidence, and focus in the face of adversity became a significant challenge for him.

6. Injuries and Health Issues: Throughout his NBA career, McDaniels also encountered significant injuries and health issues that further complicated his transition. Injuries can disrupt an athlete's development, hinder their progress, and affect their performance on the court. McDaniels had to cope with injuries that limited his playing time, hampered his ability to perform at his best, and interrupted his development as a player. Overcoming these setbacks and

maintaining a positive outlook in the face of adversity was a crucial aspect of McDaniels' journey.

Despite the initial promise McDaniels showed, the challenges of transitioning to the NBA proved formidable. In the following sections, we will delve into the struggles McDaniels faced, the impact of injuries and health issues on his career, and the lessons that can be gleaned from his experiences as a number 1 draft pick.

Struggles with injuries and inconsistency in the league

Jim McDaniels, despite his initial promise and high expectations as the number 1 draft pick, encountered significant struggles throughout his NBA career. One of the most significant challenges he faced was the burden of injuries and inconsistency, which affected his performance and hindered his ability to reach his full potential. In this section, we will explore McDaniels' struggles with injuries and inconsistency in the league, examining their impact on his career and the lessons that can be learned from his experiences.

1. The Impact of Injuries: Injuries can be a career-altering factor for any athlete, and McDaniels was no exception. Throughout his NBA journey, he faced a series of injuries that disrupted his playing time, impeded his development, and hindered his on-court performance. These injuries included sprained ankles, knee problems, and other ailments that prevented McDaniels from consistently showcasing his skills and contributing to his team's success. We will delve into the specific injuries McDaniels faced, their long-term effects, and how they shaped his career trajectory.

2. Inconsistency and Its Consequences: Inconsistency plagued McDaniels throughout his NBA career. While he

showed flashes of brilliance and exhibited the potential to be a dominant force on the court, his performances were often marred by inconsistency. McDaniels would have games where he would display his scoring ability, rebounding prowess, and shot-blocking skills, only to follow them up with lackluster performances. This inconsistency not only affected his individual statistics but also had an impact on his team's success and his standing within the league. We will examine the factors contributing to McDaniels' inconsistency and the challenges he faced in maintaining a high level of performance.

3. Mental and Emotional Toll: Dealing with injuries and inconsistency can take a significant toll on an athlete's mental and emotional well-being. McDaniels faced the frustrations of being unable to consistently perform at his best due to injuries and the resulting inconsistency. The constant cycle of rehabilitation, setbacks, and doubts about his abilities can be mentally and emotionally draining. McDaniels had to navigate the mental challenges of staying motivated, maintaining confidence in his abilities, and overcoming the setbacks caused by injuries and inconsistency. We will explore the psychological impact of these struggles and the strategies McDaniels employed to cope with the mental and emotional toll.

4. Adapting Playing Style and Adjusting Expectations: In response to his injuries and struggles with inconsistency, McDaniels had to adapt his playing style and adjust his expectations. He had to find ways to contribute to his team's success despite physical limitations and inconsistent performances. McDaniels had to refine his skills, develop alternative approaches to the game, and adapt his role within the team to maximize his impact. We will analyze the adjustments McDaniels made and how they influenced his career trajectory.

5. Lessons Learned: Despite the challenges he faced, McDaniels' struggles with injuries and inconsistency offer valuable lessons for aspiring athletes and fans alike. His experiences highlight the importance of perseverance, resilience, and adaptability in the face of adversity. McDaniels' journey serves as a reminder that setbacks and obstacles are an inherent part of any professional career, and how one responds to those challenges can ultimately determine their success. We will draw upon McDaniels' experiences to extract these valuable lessons and provide insights that can be applied not only to the world of basketball but to life in general.

As we delve into McDaniels' struggles with injuries and inconsistency, we will gain a deeper understanding of the difficulties he faced, the impact of these challenges on his career, and the resilience he displayed in the face of adversity. Through McDaniels' story, we will uncover the complexities of navigating an NBA career and the lessons that can be gleaned from his journey.

The decision to retire and the aftermath of his career

Jim McDaniels' basketball career was marked by struggles, injuries, and inconsistency. In this section, we will explore the decision that ultimately led to McDaniels' retirement from professional basketball and the aftermath of his career. We will examine the factors that contributed to his retirement, the impact it had on his life, and the legacy he left behind.

1. The Turning Point: For McDaniels, the decision to retire from professional basketball was not an easy one. After years of battling injuries and facing challenges on and off the court, McDaniels reached a turning point in his career. We will delve into the specific events and circumstances that led McDaniels to contemplate retirement and the factors he considered in making this life-altering decision.

2. Physical and Mental Considerations: Retirement decisions in professional sports are often influenced by a combination of physical and mental factors. In McDaniels' case, his injuries and the toll they took on his body played a significant role in his decision-making process. We will explore the extent of McDaniels' physical ailments, the impact they had on his ability to compete at a high level, and the implications they had for his long-term health.

Additionally, we will examine the mental aspects of McDaniels' decision, including the emotional toll of prolonged struggles and the mental preparation required to transition away from a career that had defined his identity.

3. Life After Basketball: Retirement from professional sports can be a challenging transition for athletes. McDaniels faced the daunting task of carving out a new path after leaving the NBA. We will explore the various endeavors McDaniels pursued after retiring from basketball, including his professional and personal pursuits. From coaching and mentoring young players to engaging in community initiatives, we will examine how McDaniels sought to make a positive impact beyond his playing days.

4. Legacy and Reflections: Despite the difficulties he faced during his career, McDaniels' legacy extends beyond his on-court accomplishments. We will reflect on McDaniels' impact on the game of basketball and his enduring influence on future generations of players. Additionally, we will explore McDaniels' own reflections on his career, including his thoughts on the challenges he encountered, the decisions he made, and the lessons he learned along the way.

5. Lessons Learned: The decision to retire from professional basketball and the aftermath of McDaniels' career offer valuable lessons and insights. McDaniels'

journey serves as a reminder of the importance of self-care, the need to make difficult decisions when faced with adversity, and the resilience required to navigate life's challenges. We will draw upon McDaniels' experiences to extract these valuable lessons and provide perspectives that can be applied not only to the world of sports but to life in general.

By examining McDaniels' decision to retire and the aftermath of his career, we gain a deeper understanding of the complexities of an athlete's journey and the impact of pivotal life decisions. McDaniels' story serves as a testament to the strength of character and the ability to adapt to new phases of life.

Chapter 4: Dwight Jones, picked in 1973, retired in 1983

The story of Dwight Jones' journey from college to the NBA

Dwight Jones' path from college basketball to the NBA was a unique and compelling journey. In this section, we will explore the key moments, challenges, and successes that shaped Jones' career. From his early days in college to his eventual selection as the number one draft pick, we will delve into the story behind Dwight Jones' rise to the professional ranks.

1. Early Beginnings: To understand Dwight Jones' journey, we must first delve into his early beginnings in basketball. We will explore his formative years, including his introduction to the sport, his development as a player, and the early signs of his talent and potential. From playing high school basketball to catching the attention of college recruiters, we will trace Jones' path towards becoming a highly sought-after prospect.

2. College Years: Jones' college years were a pivotal period in his basketball career. We will examine his decision to attend the University of Houston and the impact it had on his development as a player. We will delve into his college basketball career, including his standout performances,

memorable moments, and contributions to the success of the Houston Cougars. Additionally, we will explore the recognition and accolades Jones received during his college tenure, which further solidified his status as a top prospect.

3. Rising Expectations: As Jones' college career progressed, so did the expectations surrounding his future in the NBA. We will explore how his performances on the court and his reputation as a dominant force in college basketball led to heightened anticipation and projections of his success at the professional level. We will delve into the media attention, draft speculation, and discussions surrounding Jones' potential as a number one draft pick.

4. The NBA Draft: The NBA draft is a crucial moment for any aspiring player, and Jones' selection as the number one pick in 1973 was a defining moment in his career. We will examine the circumstances leading up to the draft, the factors that influenced the decision to select Jones as the top pick, and the reactions from fans, analysts, and the basketball community. Additionally, we will explore the immediate impact of Jones' selection and the expectations placed upon him as the number one draft pick.

5. Transitioning to the NBA: Transitioning from college basketball to the NBA presents its own set of challenges. We will delve into the adjustments Jones had to

make, both on and off the court, as he entered the professional ranks. From adapting to the faster pace and physicality of the NBA game to navigating the dynamics of a professional team, we will explore the hurdles Jones faced during this transitional period.

6. Moments of Success: Despite the challenges, Jones experienced notable moments of success during his NBA career. We will highlight some of his standout performances, memorable games, and contributions to his team's success. From his scoring prowess to his rebounding abilities, we will examine the skills and attributes that made Jones a formidable force on the court.

By tracing Dwight Jones' journey from college to the NBA, we gain a deeper understanding of the challenges and triumphs he encountered along the way. His story serves as a testament to the dedication, perseverance, and talent required to navigate the competitive landscape of professional basketball. Ultimately, Jones' journey provides valuable insights into the path of an elite athlete and the pursuit of greatness in the NBA.

Challenges faced as a number 1 pick in a highly competitive era

Dwight Jones' journey as the number one draft pick in the highly competitive era of the NBA presented its own unique set of challenges. In this section, we will explore the obstacles and pressures Jones faced as a top selection in a league filled with exceptional talent. From the weight of expectations to the intense competition on the court, we will delve into the challenges that shaped Jones' career and left a lasting impact on his legacy.

1. The Burden of Expectations: As the number one pick, Dwight Jones entered the NBA with enormous expectations. We will examine the weight of these expectations and how they affected Jones' mindset, performance, and overall career trajectory. From the scrutiny of the media to the pressure to live up to the hype, we will explore the psychological and emotional toll that comes with being the top selection in the draft.

2. Competing Against Legends: The era in which Jones played was filled with legendary players who defined the game. We will highlight some of the notable opponents Jones faced and the challenges of competing against such iconic figures. From going head-to-head with dominant centers like Kareem Abdul-Jabbar and Bill Walton to facing

off against skilled forwards and guards, we will explore the level of competition Jones encountered on a nightly basis.

3. Physical Demands and Rigors: The NBA is known for its physicality and demands on players' bodies. We will delve into the physical challenges Jones faced as a number one pick, including the grueling schedule, intense training regimens, and the toll of injuries. We will explore how these factors impacted Jones' performance, longevity in the league, and overall well-being.

4. Team Expectations and Dynamics: As a number one draft pick, Jones was not only expected to excel individually but also to elevate the performance of his team. We will examine the dynamics between Jones and his teammates, coaches, and front office personnel. From the pressures of leading a team to the complexities of fitting into existing systems, we will analyze the challenges Jones faced in fulfilling the team's expectations.

5. Media and Public Scrutiny: Being a high-profile player, Jones was subjected to intense media scrutiny and public judgment. We will explore how the media's perception of Jones influenced his career and public image. From the portrayal of his performances to the narratives surrounding his success or perceived failures, we will analyze the impact of media scrutiny on Jones' journey as a number one pick.

6. Mental Resilience and Coping Strategies: Navigating the challenges of being a number one pick required mental resilience and coping strategies. We will explore the ways in which Jones dealt with the pressures and setbacks he encountered. From maintaining focus and motivation to developing mental fortitude, we will examine the strategies Jones employed to overcome the challenges he faced as a top draft pick.

By examining the challenges Dwight Jones faced as the number one pick in a highly competitive era, we gain a deeper understanding of the complexities and pressures of professional basketball. Jones' story serves as a reminder that even the most talented and highly touted players must overcome numerous obstacles to succeed in such a fiercely competitive environment. Ultimately, Jones' journey sheds light on the resilience and determination required to navigate the challenges and leave a lasting legacy in the NBA.

Moments of success and recognition in the league

While Dwight Jones faced numerous challenges as the number one pick in a highly competitive era, he also experienced moments of success and recognition during his NBA career. In this section, we will explore the highlights and achievements that showcased Jones' talent and affirmed his place in the league. From memorable performances to notable accomplishments, we will delve into the moments that defined Jones' career and solidified his reputation as a skilled player.

1. Breakout Seasons and Statistical Achievements: We will examine the seasons in which Jones truly shined, showcasing his skills and making significant contributions to his team. We will analyze his statistical achievements, such as scoring averages, rebounds, and blocks, and how these numbers reflect his impact on the court. From double-double performances to standout games against formidable opponents, we will highlight the individual accomplishments that marked Jones' career.

2. All-Star Appearances and Recognition: Jones' talent and contributions to the game earned him recognition on the grand stage of the NBA All-Star Game. We will explore the seasons in which he received All-Star honors, examining the selection process and the significance of being

chosen among the league's elite players. We will delve into his performances during these All-Star games, showcasing his skills in a competitive and star-studded environment.

3. Playoff Performances and Postseason Success: The NBA playoffs provide a stage for players to showcase their abilities and compete for championships. We will analyze Jones' performances in the postseason, examining his impact on his team's success and his ability to elevate his game when it mattered most. From clutch moments to memorable playoff series, we will highlight the ways in which Jones contributed to his team's playoff runs and left a mark on the postseason.

4. Individual Awards and Accolades: Beyond All-Star selections, Jones received recognition for his achievements through various individual awards and accolades. We will explore the honors he received, such as Player of the Week or Month, and how these acknowledgments reflected his talent and impact on the court. We will also examine any team or conference awards that Jones earned throughout his career, further solidifying his reputation as a respected player in the league.

5. Contributions to Team Success: Jones' success extended beyond individual achievements, as he played a crucial role in his team's accomplishments during his career.

We will delve into the teams he played for and analyze his contributions to their success, whether it was leading his team in scoring, providing a defensive presence, or serving as a leader on and off the court. We will highlight key moments where Jones' impact was instrumental in his team's achievements.

6. Legacy and Influence: Jones' moments of success and recognition have a lasting impact on his legacy in the NBA. We will explore how his accomplishments shaped his place in basketball history and influenced future players. We will analyze the ways in which Jones' style of play, skills, and contributions have had a lasting impact on the game, both in terms of on-court performance and off-court influence.

By examining Dwight Jones' moments of success and recognition in the league, we gain a deeper appreciation for his talent and contributions to the game of basketball. These moments showcase his abilities and highlight the impact he had on his teams and the league as a whole. Jones' story serves as a reminder that even in the face of challenges, moments of triumph and recognition can define a player's career and leave a lasting legacy in the NBA.

Coping with the eventual decline and retiring from professional basketball

Dwight Jones' journey in the NBA was not without its challenges, and like many athletes, he had to face the eventual decline of his career and make the difficult decision to retire from professional basketball. In this section, we will explore the various factors and emotions involved in coping with the end of a successful career. From the physical toll on the body to the emotional adjustments required, we will delve into Jones' experiences as he navigated the transition out of the game he loved.

1. Physical Challenges and Declining Performance: As athletes age and accumulate years of wear and tear on their bodies, they often experience a decline in physical abilities. We will examine how Jones' athleticism and skills were affected by factors such as injuries, aging, and the natural decline in performance that comes with time. We will explore the physical challenges he faced on the court and how they impacted his ability to compete at the highest level.

2. Mental and Emotional Adjustment: Retiring from professional basketball is not only a physical transition but also an emotional one. We will explore the mental and emotional challenges that Jones encountered as he confronted the reality of his career winding down. From the

psychological impact of stepping away from a lifelong passion to the loss of identity and purpose that can accompany retirement, we will delve into the emotional journey Jones embarked upon during this period.

3. Life After Basketball: Retirement from professional basketball marked a significant turning point in Jones' life. We will examine the adjustments he had to make as he transitioned into a post-basketball career and sought to find new avenues for fulfillment and success. We will explore the paths he pursued, such as coaching, entrepreneurship, or involvement in the basketball community, and how these endeavors allowed him to stay connected to the game while exploring new opportunities.

4. Legacy and Reflections: The end of a career prompts athletes to reflect on their accomplishments and the mark they have left on the sport. We will delve into Jones' reflections on his career, examining his perspective on the highs and lows, the challenges faced, and the impact he made during his time in the NBA. We will explore how he chose to preserve and share his basketball legacy and how his experiences shaped his outlook on life beyond the game.

5. Transitioning to a New Chapter: Retirement from professional basketball represents a new chapter in an athlete's life, and we will explore how Jones embraced this

transition. We will examine the personal growth and reinvention he experienced as he redirected his energy and passion toward new endeavors. We will also highlight any contributions he made to the basketball community or society at large during this phase of his life.

6. Lessons and Insights: Through Jones' experiences in coping with the decline and retirement from professional basketball, we can glean valuable lessons and insights. We will explore the wisdom he gained from navigating this challenging period and how it shaped his perspective on life, success, and the pursuit of personal fulfillment. We will also discuss the broader implications of retirement for athletes and the importance of planning and support systems during this transition.

Coping with the eventual decline and retiring from professional basketball is a formidable task that requires physical, mental, and emotional resilience. Dwight Jones' journey provides us with a window into the realities faced by athletes when their playing days come to an end. By exploring the challenges he encountered and the strategies he employed to navigate this transition, we can gain a deeper understanding of the complex and multifaceted process of retiring from a career in professional sports.

Chapter 5: Bob Boozer, picked in 1960, retired in 1971

Bob Boozer's rise to prominence in college basketball

Bob Boozer's journey to becoming a number one draft pick in the NBA was shaped by his remarkable rise to prominence in college basketball. In this section, we will explore Boozer's early years, his college career, and the factors that contributed to his emergence as a highly sought-after prospect. From his humble beginnings to his dominance on the collegiate stage, we will delve into the captivating story of Boozer's rise to fame.

1. Early Life and Basketball Beginnings: To understand Boozer's rise to prominence, we must first explore his early life and the foundation upon which his basketball career was built. We will delve into his childhood, family background, and the early experiences that ignited his passion for the game. From pickup games in the neighborhood to organized basketball in school, we will trace Boozer's early steps in the sport and the influences that shaped his development.

2. High School Success and Recognition: Boozer's talent began to attract attention during his high school years. We will delve into his achievements on the high school

basketball scene, including standout performances, accolades, and the impact he made on his team. We will explore the recruitment process and the interest shown by college programs as Boozer's star continued to rise.

3. College Choice and Impact: Boozer's college decision played a pivotal role in his rise to prominence. We will explore the factors that influenced his choice of university and how it set the stage for his collegiate success. We will delve into his experiences on the college basketball court, highlighting his contributions to the team and the impact he made on the program. From memorable games to individual accomplishments, we will paint a vivid picture of Boozer's college career.

4. Dominance in Collegiate Basketball: Boozer's rise to prominence reached new heights during his college years, as he established himself as one of the premier players in the nation. We will examine his statistical achievements, his impact on the team's success, and the moments that solidified his reputation as a dominant force on the court. We will also explore his playing style, skills, and the qualities that set him apart from his peers.

5. National Recognition and Awards: Boozer's exceptional performances in college basketball did not go unnoticed. We will delve into the national recognition he

received, including All-American selections, conference honors, and other prestigious awards. We will examine the impact of these accolades on Boozer's reputation and how they further elevated his status as a top prospect for the NBA.

6. Legacy and Influence: Beyond his individual accomplishments, Boozer's rise to prominence in college basketball left a lasting legacy. We will explore the influence he had on the game and the impact he made on future generations of players. We will examine his contributions to the sport both on and off the court, including his sportsmanship, leadership qualities, and the values he embodied as a college basketball star.

7. Reflections on College Career: Throughout this section, we will include Boozer's own reflections on his college career. We will delve into interviews, quotes, and personal accounts that offer insights into his mindset, motivations, and experiences during this transformative period of his life. By hearing directly from Boozer, we will gain a deeper understanding of his journey and the significance of his rise to prominence in college basketball.

Bob Boozer's rise to prominence in college basketball set the stage for his selection as a number one draft pick in the NBA. By exploring his early years, his college career, and the impact he made on the game, we can appreciate the remarkable journey that led him to the pinnacle of basketball success.

The excitement and expectations surrounding his number 1 selection

When Bob Boozer was selected as the number one pick in the 1960 NBA Draft, the basketball world buzzed with excitement and high expectations. In this section, we will delve into the anticipation and enthusiasm surrounding Boozer's selection, exploring the factors that contributed to the excitement, the reactions from fans and experts, and the weight of expectations placed upon him as the top pick. From the draft day drama to the hopes and dreams that accompanied his selection, we will unravel the captivating story of the excitement and expectations surrounding Bob Boozer's number one selection.

1. The NBA Draft Process: Before we delve into Boozer's selection, it is important to provide an overview of the NBA draft process during that era. We will explore how the draft worked, the significance of being a number one pick, and the historical context of previous top selections. By understanding the draft landscape of the time, we can better appreciate the magnitude of Boozer's selection.

2. Pre-Draft Buzz and Speculation: As the draft approached, anticipation built, and speculations ran rampant about who would be the number one pick. We will examine the pre-draft buzz surrounding Boozer, including

the media coverage, scouting reports, and expert opinions. We will delve into the factors that made Boozer a top prospect and the qualities that set him apart from other players in the draft class.

3. Draft Day Drama: The moment finally arrived on draft day when Bob Boozer's name was called as the number one pick. We will recreate the atmosphere and drama of that day, describing the scene, the reactions from fans and experts, and the emotions experienced by Boozer and those close to him. We will highlight the significance of his selection and the immediate impact it had on his life and career.

4. Fan and Media Expectations: Following his selection, the expectations placed upon Boozer were sky-high. We will delve into the reactions of fans and the media, capturing the excitement and anticipation surrounding his potential as a player. We will analyze the reasons behind the heightened expectations and how they affected Boozer's perception and the pressure he faced entering the NBA.

5. Franchise and Team Expectations: Boozer's selection as the number one pick carried significant expectations not only for him personally but also for the franchise that drafted him. We will explore the expectations of the team, the role Boozer was expected to play, and the

impact his success would have on the franchise's fortunes. We will also examine the support and resources provided to Boozer to help him meet those expectations.

6. Comparisons and Projections: Being the number one pick in the draft often invites comparisons to past greats and projections of future success. We will explore the comparisons made between Boozer and other notable players, both past and present, examining how these comparisons influenced the expectations placed upon him. We will also delve into the projections made by experts and how they shaped the narrative surrounding Boozer's potential.

7. Managing Expectations and Dealing with Pressure: The weight of expectations and the pressure to live up to the number one pick status can be overwhelming for any player. We will delve into how Boozer managed these expectations, the strategies he employed to cope with the pressure, and the support he received from his teammates, coaches, and mentors. We will highlight the mental and emotional aspects of navigating high expectations in professional basketball.

8. Reflections on the Expectations: Throughout this section, we will include Boozer's own reflections on the expectations placed upon him as the number one pick. We will delve into interviews, quotes, and personal accounts that

offer insights into his mindset, the challenges he faced, and how he dealt with the pressure. By hearing directly from Boozer, we can gain a deeper understanding of the excitement and expectations he experienced during this pivotal time in his career.

Bob Boozer's selection as the number one pick in the 1960 NBA Draft generated tremendous excitement and carried significant expectations. By exploring the pre-draft buzz, the draft day drama, and the reactions from fans and experts, we can unravel the captivating story of the anticipation and pressure that accompanied Boozer's number one selection.

Challenges faced in adjusting to the NBA game

After being selected as the number one pick in the 1960 NBA Draft, Bob Boozer faced numerous challenges in adapting to the professional game. In this section, we will explore the obstacles and adjustments Boozer encountered as he transitioned from college basketball to the NBA. From the differences in playing style and physicality to the demands of the professional level, we will delve into the unique challenges Boozer faced and how he navigated them.

1. Style of Play: One of the most significant adjustments for Boozer was adapting to the style of play in the NBA. We will examine the differences between college and professional basketball, including the faster pace, increased physicality, and strategic nuances. We will explore how Boozer had to refine his skills and adapt his game to thrive in the NBA environment.

2. Physical Demands: The NBA presented a whole new level of physicality compared to college basketball. We will delve into the challenges Boozer faced in adjusting to the size, strength, and athleticism of professional players. We will discuss the physical demands of the NBA game and how Boozer worked to improve his strength, endurance, and overall conditioning to compete at the highest level.

3. Competition and Talent Level: As the number one pick, Boozer entered a league filled with exceptional talent. We will explore the caliber of players he faced night in and night out, including seasoned veterans and established stars. We will analyze the challenges Boozer encountered in matching up against elite opponents and how he worked to elevate his game to compete at their level.

4. Defensive Adjustments: Defense is an integral part of success in the NBA, and Boozer had to adapt to the defensive schemes and strategies employed by opposing teams. We will delve into the defensive challenges he faced, including guarding versatile opponents and understanding complex defensive rotations. We will also discuss how Boozer honed his defensive skills and worked to become a solid defender in the league.

5. Role and Expectations: As the number one pick, Boozer was expected to make an immediate impact and contribute significantly to his team's success. We will examine the expectations placed upon him and the challenges of fulfilling those expectations. We will discuss how Boozer navigated his role on the team, the adjustments he had to make to fit into the system, and the pressure to perform at a high level.

6. Coaching and Mentorship: Boozer's adjustment to the NBA was facilitated by the guidance of his coaches and the mentorship of experienced teammates. We will explore the influence of his coaches on his development, their strategies for helping him adapt to the professional game, and the mentorship he received from veteran players. We will highlight the crucial role coaching and mentorship played in Boozer's transition.

7. Psychological Adjustments: The mental aspect of transitioning to the NBA should not be overlooked. We will discuss the psychological challenges Boozer faced, such as the pressure to succeed, the scrutiny from media and fans, and the mental resilience required to bounce back from setbacks. We will explore how Boozer managed these psychological challenges and maintained a positive mindset to overcome adversity.

8. Learning from Setbacks: Adapting to the NBA often involves facing setbacks and overcoming obstacles. We will examine the setbacks Boozer encountered during his early NBA career, such as injuries, slumps in performance, and adjusting to new coaching strategies. We will discuss how he learned from these setbacks, made necessary adjustments, and used them as opportunities for growth and improvement.

By exploring the challenges Boozer faced in adjusting to the NBA game, we gain a deeper understanding of the complexities of transitioning from college to the professional level. Despite the hurdles he encountered, Boozer's journey is a testament to his resilience, adaptability, and determination to succeed in the face of adversity.

Reflections on his career and legacy in the league

In this section, we will delve into the reflections of Bob Boozer himself on his career in the NBA and the lasting legacy he left behind. We will explore Boozer's thoughts and insights on his accomplishments, challenges, and the impact he made on the league and future generations of players. Through interviews, personal anecdotes, and historical analysis, we will gain a deeper understanding of Boozer's career and the mark he left on professional basketball.

1. Personal Fulfillment: We will begin by examining Boozer's personal reflections on his career and how he felt about his overall achievements. We will explore his sense of fulfillment, satisfaction, and any regrets he may have had. We will discuss the moments that brought him the most joy and the challenges that shaped his journey.

2. Career Highlights: Boozer's career was filled with notable highlights and accomplishments. We will delve into his most memorable performances, record-breaking moments, and significant milestones. We will explore the impact these achievements had on his confidence, reputation, and legacy within the league.

3. Contributions to the Game: Boozer's influence extended beyond his individual accomplishments. We will discuss his contributions to the game of basketball, both on

and off the court. We will explore his playing style, skills, and basketball IQ, as well as the ways in which he impacted the strategies and tactics employed by teams during his era.

4. Team Dynamics and Relationships: Basketball is a team sport, and Boozer's success was influenced by his relationships with teammates and coaches. We will examine Boozer's reflections on his interactions with teammates, the camaraderie he experienced, and the role he played within the team dynamics. We will also explore the impact of his relationships on his individual performance and overall career.

5. Impact on Future Generations: Boozer's legacy extends beyond his playing years. We will explore how his career and success paved the way for future generations of players. We will discuss his influence on younger athletes, the impact he had on the development of the game, and the ways in which his style of play or approach to the game inspired others.

6. Off-Court Contributions: Beyond his on-court achievements, Boozer's life and career may have included off-court contributions that left a lasting impact. We will explore any philanthropic endeavors, community involvement, or leadership roles Boozer took on during or after his playing days. We will discuss how his actions

outside of the game shaped his legacy and the way he is remembered.

7. Legacy and Place in Basketball History: We will conclude this section by examining Boozer's legacy and his place in basketball history. We will analyze how he is remembered within the context of his era, his impact on the teams he played for, and his standing among his peers. We will also discuss how his career has been evaluated by historians, fans, and basketball experts.

By reflecting on Boozer's career and the legacy he left behind, we gain a comprehensive understanding of his contributions to the game and the mark he made on professional basketball. His journey serves as a testament to his skill, dedication, and the lasting impact a player can have beyond their playing days.

Chapter 6: Exploring the common themes and lessons

Analyzing the shared experiences of these number 1 draft picks

In this section, we will delve into the shared experiences of the number 1 draft picks from 1960 to 1980. By analyzing their stories, we can uncover common themes, challenges, and lessons that emerged from their journeys. Through a comprehensive examination of their careers, we will gain insights into the pressures of being a top pick, the expectations placed upon them, and the factors that contributed to their struggles. By identifying these shared experiences, we can extract valuable lessons for future generations of players and gain a deeper understanding of the fragile nature of success in professional basketball.

1. Expectations and Pressure: One common theme among these number 1 draft picks is the immense pressure they faced as highly anticipated rookies. We will analyze the expectations placed upon them, both internally and externally, and how these expectations affected their performance and mental well-being. We will explore the weight of being labeled as the top pick and the challenges of living up to those expectations.

2. Adaptation to the NBA: Transitioning from college basketball to the NBA presents its own set of challenges. We will examine how these players navigated the shift in competition, style of play, and level of physicality. We will discuss the adjustments they had to make, the learning curves they encountered, and the impact these transitions had on their careers.

3. Coping with Setbacks and Disappointments: Another common thread among these number 1 picks is the presence of setbacks, disappointments, and obstacles along their paths. We will analyze how they dealt with injuries, performance slumps, and off-court challenges. We will explore the mental and emotional toll these setbacks had on their careers and their ability to bounce back or persevere.

4. External Factors and Support Systems: The influence of external factors and support systems cannot be underestimated. We will examine the role of coaches, teammates, family, and friends in the lives and careers of these players. We will explore how positive or negative influences shaped their experiences and impacted their ability to overcome challenges.

5. Lessons in Resilience and Determination: Despite the struggles and unfulfilled potential, these number 1 draft picks demonstrated remarkable resilience and

determination. We will analyze their ability to persevere in the face of adversity, their willingness to work through challenges, and the lessons we can learn from their resilience.

6. The Toll of Unfulfilled Expectations: The weight of unfulfilled expectations can have a significant impact on a player's career and personal well-being. We will examine the emotional toll experienced by these number 1 picks as they fell short of the lofty expectations set for them. We will discuss the psychological effects and the ways in which these experiences shaped their lives beyond basketball.

7. Finding Meaning and Redemption: In some cases, these number 1 draft picks were able to find meaning and redemption in their careers, even if they didn't meet the initial expectations. We will explore how they redefined success, found purpose beyond the court, or rebuilt their lives after basketball. We will analyze the lessons we can learn from their journeys of self-discovery and reinvention.

By analyzing the shared experiences of these number 1 draft picks, we can identify recurring themes, challenges, and lessons that provide valuable insights into the nature of success and the realities of professional basketball. Their stories serve as cautionary tales, sources of inspiration, and reminders of the importance of resilience, adaptability, and personal growth in the face of adversity.

The impact of external factors on their careers

In this section, we will examine the influence of external factors on the careers of the number 1 draft picks from 1960 to 1980. While individual talent and dedication play a significant role in success, external circumstances can shape a player's trajectory and impact their ability to fulfill their potential. By analyzing these external factors, we can gain a deeper understanding of the complex interplay between personal circumstances, team dynamics, and broader social and cultural influences. Through the exploration of these factors, we can identify the challenges faced by these number 1 picks and the lessons we can learn from their experiences.

1. Team Culture and Dynamics: The environment within an NBA team can significantly impact a player's career. We will analyze the team cultures and dynamics that these number 1 draft picks encountered. This includes examining the coaching styles, teammate relationships, and organizational structures that either supported or hindered their development. We will explore how team dynamics influenced their performance, confidence, and overall career trajectory.

2. Coaching and Mentorship: The role of coaches and mentors cannot be overstated in a player's journey. We will

explore the impact of coaching on the number 1 draft picks, examining how coaching philosophies, strategies, and personal relationships shaped their careers. We will analyze the influence of mentors who provided guidance, support, and constructive criticism, and how these relationships affected the players' growth and development.

3. Surrounding Talent and Team Success: The level of talent and success of a player's teammates can have a significant impact on their individual performance and recognition. We will examine how the surrounding talent influenced the number 1 draft picks' opportunities, role within the team, and overall success. We will analyze the challenges faced by players who were surrounded by weaker or mismatched teammates, as well as those who thrived alongside a talented supporting cast.

4. Media and Public Perception: The media plays a crucial role in shaping public perception and expectations of players. We will explore how media coverage influenced the number 1 draft picks' careers, examining the narratives that were created around them and how these narratives affected their confidence, public image, and endorsement opportunities. We will analyze the pressures and scrutiny that came with being in the spotlight and the ways in which

media perception impacted their performance on and off the court.

5. Social and Cultural Context: The social and cultural context in which these number 1 draft picks played cannot be overlooked. We will examine the racial dynamics of the era and how they affected these players' experiences. We will analyze the challenges and opportunities presented by societal attitudes, prejudices, and evolving cultural norms. By exploring the social and cultural context, we can gain a deeper understanding of the external pressures and challenges these players faced.

6. Economic Factors and Contract Negotiations: Financial considerations and contract negotiations can have a significant impact on a player's career and decisions. We will explore how economic factors, such as contract disputes, financial instability, and the evolving nature of player compensation, influenced the number 1 draft picks' decisions and career trajectories. We will analyze how financial pressures and contractual obligations impacted their performance and long-term prospects.

7. Personal and Family Circumstances: Personal and family circumstances can also play a crucial role in a player's career. We will examine the impact of personal challenges, such as injuries, health issues, or personal tragedies, on

these number 1 draft picks. We will explore how personal circumstances affected their mindset, motivation, and ability to perform at their best.

By analyzing the impact of external factors on the careers of these number 1 draft picks, we can gain insights into the complex web of influences that shape a player's journey. Understanding these factors can provide valuable lessons for future generations of players, coaches, and organizations in creating supportive environments that allow players to thrive. Furthermore, it sheds light on the broader social, cultural, and economic forces that shape the world of professional basketball.

Lessons learned from their struggles and disappointments

Introduction: In this section, we will delve into the lessons learned from the struggles and disappointments faced by the number 1 draft picks from 1960 to 1980. While these players had tremendous talent and potential, their careers were not without obstacles and setbacks. By examining their challenges, we can uncover valuable insights and lessons that can be applied to both basketball and life in general. These lessons will offer guidance and inspiration to aspiring athletes, coaches, and individuals striving to overcome adversity and achieve their goals.

1. Resilience and Perseverance: One of the fundamental lessons we learn from these number 1 draft picks is the importance of resilience and perseverance. Despite facing various challenges, including injuries, criticism, and setbacks, these players demonstrated the ability to bounce back and continue pursuing their dreams. We will explore how they developed mental toughness, maintained focus, and found the inner strength to overcome adversity. Their stories serve as a reminder that setbacks are part of the journey, and it is how we respond to them that defines our character and potential for success.

2. Managing Expectations: The number 1 draft picks in this era often faced sky-high expectations from fans, media, and even themselves. We will examine the lessons they learned about managing expectations and the pressure that comes with being at the top. From coping with the weight of lofty predictions to handling the burden of representing an entire franchise, they provide valuable insights on maintaining a balanced mindset and staying focused on personal growth and development.

3. Embracing Growth and Adaptability: The struggles and disappointments experienced by these number 1 draft picks highlight the importance of continuous growth and adaptability. We will explore how they learned to embrace change, refine their skills, and adapt their game to overcome challenges. Whether it was adjusting to a new system, improving weaknesses, or expanding their skill set, these players exemplify the value of being open to learning and evolving as individuals and athletes.

4. Finding Support Systems: A common theme among the number 1 draft picks is the significance of having a strong support system. We will examine the lessons learned about the importance of mentors, coaches, teammates, and family members in navigating challenges and maintaining motivation. Their stories emphasize the value of seeking

guidance, building positive relationships, and surrounding oneself with individuals who believe in their potential.

5. Balancing Individual Goals and Team Success: The experiences of these number 1 draft picks demonstrate the delicate balance between individual aspirations and team success. We will explore the lessons they learned about collaboration, leadership, and the importance of contributing to the collective objectives of the team. Their stories highlight the significance of finding a balance between personal ambitions and the greater good, fostering a team-first mentality while still striving for personal excellence.

6. Resilience in the Face of Adversity: Many of these number 1 draft picks encountered significant obstacles that tested their resilience. We will examine their stories of resilience in the face of injuries, setbacks, and disappointments. By exploring their experiences, we can learn valuable lessons about maintaining a positive mindset, staying committed to the journey, and turning setbacks into opportunities for growth.

7. Life Beyond Basketball: Lastly, we will explore the lessons these number 1 draft picks learned about life beyond basketball. While their careers in the NBA may have had their share of struggles and disappointments, their stories continue to inspire beyond the court. We will examine how

they transitioned into new phases of their lives, pursued diverse interests, and made positive impacts in their communities. Their journeys offer valuable insights into resilience, adaptability, and finding fulfillment beyond the realm of professional sports.

Conclusion: The struggles and disappointments faced by the number 1 draft picks from 1960 to 1980 provide invaluable lessons that extend beyond the basketball court. From resilience and perseverance to managing expectations and embracing growth, their stories offer guidance and inspiration for individuals navigating their own challenges and striving for success. By analyzing their experiences, we can glean valuable insights that can be applied to various aspects of life, making this chapter a source of motivation and learning for athletes, coaches, and individuals seeking to overcome adversity and achieve their goals.

Reflections on the challenges faced by these players

Introduction: In this section, we will reflect on the challenges faced by the number 1 draft picks from 1960 to 1980. These players, despite their tremendous talent and potential, encountered numerous obstacles throughout their careers. By examining their challenges, we can gain a deeper understanding of the difficulties they faced and the lessons that emerged from their experiences. This reflection will provide insight into the realities of professional basketball during that era and shed light on the resilience, determination, and personal growth required to overcome adversity.

1. Physical Demands and Injury Challenges: One of the significant challenges faced by these players was the physical demands of the game and the injuries they encountered. We will reflect on the toll that high-intensity play took on their bodies and how injuries impacted their careers. From knee injuries to back problems, we will examine the physical challenges they faced and the impact these challenges had on their performance, longevity, and overall well-being.

2. The Pressure of Expectations: Being a number 1 draft pick often came with immense pressure and sky-high expectations. We will reflect on the weight of these

expectations and the psychological challenges they posed for these players. The burden of living up to the hype, meeting the lofty predictions, and carrying the hopes of a franchise can have a profound effect on an athlete's mental well-being. We will explore how these players navigated the pressure, the psychological toll it took, and the lessons they learned about managing expectations.

3. Transitioning to the NBA: Transitioning from college basketball to the NBA presented its own set of challenges for these players. We will reflect on the adjustments they had to make, both on and off the court, in terms of the pace, physicality, and level of competition. The transition to the professional ranks demanded adaptation, refinement of skills, and a steep learning curve. We will delve into their experiences, the difficulties they encountered, and the lessons they learned about resilience, patience, and the importance of a growth mindset.

4. Balancing Individual Excellence and Team Success: Striking a balance between individual brilliance and team success is a challenge that many number 1 draft picks faced. We will reflect on the delicate dynamics of team sports and how these players navigated the tension between personal goals and the greater objectives of the team. The lessons learned about collaboration, leadership, sacrifice, and

finding the right balance will be explored in the context of their experiences.

5. Media Scrutiny and Public Perception: Being in the spotlight as a number 1 draft pick comes with increased media scrutiny and public attention. We will reflect on the challenges these players faced in terms of media pressure, criticism, and public perception. The impact of media narratives, both positive and negative, on their careers and personal lives will be examined, highlighting the lessons learned about resilience, maintaining focus, and developing a strong sense of self amidst external noise.

6. Personal and Off-Court Challenges: Beyond the game itself, many of these players faced personal challenges and off-court issues that affected their careers. We will reflect on the struggles they encountered, such as financial difficulties, personal relationships, and the temptations that came with fame and success. These reflections will provide insight into the complexities of being a professional athlete and the importance of personal growth, self-discipline, and seeking support during challenging times.

7. The Role of Time and Era: Reflection on the challenges faced by these players would be incomplete without considering the context of the time and the era in which they played. We will reflect on the social, cultural, and

institutional factors that shaped their experiences, including racial dynamics, evolving playing styles, and changing expectations. This analysis will provide a broader understanding of the challenges they faced and the progress made within the NBA during this period.

Conclusion: Reflecting on the challenges faced by the number 1 draft picks from 1960 to 1980 offers valuable insights into the realities of professional basketball and the lessons that emerged from their experiences. Through physical demands, pressure, transitions, team dynamics, media scrutiny, personal challenges, and the influence of time and era, these players navigated a complex landscape. Their stories illuminate the importance of resilience, adaptability, mental fortitude, and personal growth in overcoming challenges and achieving success. By exploring these reflections, we can learn from their experiences and apply these lessons to our own lives.

Chapter 7: Impact and Aftermath
Examining the lasting impact of their underwhelming careers

Introduction: In this section, we will delve into the lasting impact of the underwhelming careers of the number 1 draft picks from 1960 to 1980. Despite the high expectations and potential they possessed, some of these players did not achieve the level of success anticipated of them. However, their careers still left a significant imprint on the basketball landscape, and their stories offer valuable lessons and insights. We will examine the factors that contributed to their underwhelming careers and explore the lasting impact they had on the NBA, the players themselves, and the wider basketball community.

1. Legacy of Unfulfilled Potential: The underwhelming careers of these number 1 draft picks left a legacy of unfulfilled potential. We will examine the reasons behind their underperformance, such as injuries, personal challenges, or the inability to meet expectations, and analyze the impact of unfulfilled potential on their individual legacies. Despite falling short of their projected success, their stories serve as a reminder of the complexities of professional sports and the challenges that can hinder even the most promising athletes.

2. Lessons for Future Generations: The underwhelming careers of these players offer valuable lessons for future generations of athletes. We will explore the lessons that can be learned from their experiences, including the importance of resilience, adaptability, humility, and self-awareness. Their stories serve as cautionary tales and provide insights into the mental, physical, and emotional demands of professional sports. By examining their underwhelming careers, we can extract valuable lessons that can inspire and guide aspiring athletes in their own journeys.

3. Influence on Draft Evaluation and Player Development: The underwhelming careers of these number 1 draft picks had a lasting impact on the evaluation of draft prospects and player development strategies. We will examine how their experiences influenced the way teams evaluate talent and make draft decisions. The lessons learned from these underperforming players have led to changes in scouting methods, emphasis on character evaluation, and the development of support systems to help players navigate the challenges they may face in their careers.

4. Impact on Franchise Building and Team Building Strategies: The underwhelming careers of these players also had implications for franchise building and team building strategies. We will analyze how their lack of success affected

the teams that selected them and explore the strategies that franchises have since adopted to build competitive teams. The experiences of these underperforming number 1 draft picks have contributed to a more comprehensive approach to team building, including the consideration of team chemistry, player fit, and the long-term development of talent.

5. Lessons for Player Support and Well-being: The underwhelming careers of these players shed light on the importance of player support and well-being. We will examine the role of coaching staff, teammates, and the organization in supporting players who may be struggling to meet expectations. Their experiences highlight the need for mental health resources, mentorship programs, and a comprehensive support system to help athletes cope with the pressures and challenges they face.

6. Impact on Perceptions of Success and Failure: The underwhelming careers of these number 1 draft picks challenge conventional notions of success and failure in professional sports. We will explore how their stories reshape our understanding of achievement and the significance of individual statistics and accolades. Their experiences remind us that success in sports is multifaceted and cannot be solely measured by individual

accomplishments. This reflection encourages a broader perspective on success, emphasizing personal growth, resilience, and the impact players have beyond their on-court performance.

7. Lasting Contributions and Redemption Stories: Despite their underwhelming careers, some of these players made lasting contributions to the game. We will highlight instances where players were able to redeem themselves or find success in other areas of the basketball industry. These redemption stories serve as sources of inspiration and illustrate the resilience and determination required to overcome setbacks. By examining the lasting contributions of these players, we acknowledge that their impact extends beyond their playing careers.

Conclusion: Examining the lasting impact of the underwhelming careers of the number 1 draft picks from 1960 to 1980 reveals valuable insights into the complexities of professional sports. Their stories offer lessons for aspiring athletes, shape draft evaluation and player development strategies, influence franchise and team building approaches, and emphasize the importance of player support and well-being. Moreover, their experiences challenge our understanding of success and failure and highlight the lasting contributions and redemption stories that can emerge from adversity. By examining the impact and aftermath of their underwhelming careers, we gain a deeper appreciation for the broader narrative of sports and the resilience of those who persevere in the face of challenges.

How these number 1 picks are remembered in basketball history

Introduction: In this section, we will explore how the number 1 draft picks from 1960 to 1980, despite their underwhelming careers, are remembered in basketball history. While their on-court performances may not have lived up to the lofty expectations placed upon them, their stories and contributions have left an indelible mark on the sport. We will examine the factors that have shaped their legacies, the narratives that surround them, and the ways in which their impact extends beyond their playing careers.

1. The Context of Their Era: To understand how these number 1 picks are remembered, it is crucial to consider the context of the era in which they played. We will provide an overview of the basketball landscape during the 1960s to 1980s, including the style of play, the level of competition, and the cultural and societal influences that shaped the perception of success and failure. This context will help illuminate the challenges and expectations faced by the number 1 picks of that time.

2. Reevaluation of Success and Failure: The underwhelming careers of these number 1 draft picks have prompted a reevaluation of success and failure in basketball. We will examine how their stories have challenged

traditional notions of achievement and the significance of individual statistics and accolades. Their legacies serve as a reminder that success is multifaceted and cannot be solely determined by on-court performance. We will explore the shifting perspectives on success in the basketball community and how it has impacted the way these players are remembered.

3. Contributions Beyond Playing Careers: While their playing careers may not have met expectations, many of these number 1 picks made significant contributions to the sport off the court. We will highlight their involvement in coaching, broadcasting, front-office roles, and philanthropy. These contributions have allowed them to shape the game in different capacities and have cemented their place in basketball history beyond their playing days. We will explore how these off-court endeavors have influenced their legacies and the broader impact they have had on the basketball community.

4. Redemption and Resilience Stories: Within the underwhelming careers of these number 1 picks, there are stories of redemption and resilience. We will examine instances where players were able to overcome adversity, reinvent themselves, or find success later in their careers. These stories of resilience resonate with fans and serve as a

testament to the human spirit and the capacity for personal growth. We will explore how these narratives of redemption and resilience have influenced the way these players are remembered and celebrated.

5. Cultural and Historical Significance: The number 1 draft picks from 1960 to 1980 hold cultural and historical significance within the basketball community. We will analyze how their careers intersected with important moments in basketball history and broader societal shifts. Their impact on the sport, despite their underwhelming performances, is a reflection of the era in which they played and the larger cultural context. We will examine the narratives and symbolism associated with these players and their lasting impact on basketball history.

6. The Influence on Future Generations: Although their careers may not have met expectations, these number 1 draft picks have influenced future generations of players. We will explore how their experiences, challenges, and legacies have served as lessons for aspiring athletes. Their stories have become cautionary tales, teaching the importance of mental fortitude, resilience, and the ability to navigate the pressures of the game. We will examine the ways in which these players have influenced the mindset and approach of young athletes striving for success in basketball.

7. Remembering the Human Element: Ultimately, how these number 1 picks are remembered in basketball history goes beyond their on-court performances. We will emphasize the human element of their stories, including their struggles, disappointments, and the personal growth they experienced throughout their careers. By recognizing their humanity and the challenges they faced, we gain a deeper understanding of their legacies and the impact they have had on the basketball community.

Conclusion: The way these number 1 draft picks from 1960 to 1980 are remembered in basketball history is a complex interplay of their on-court performances, their contributions beyond playing careers, the context of their era, and the cultural and historical significance they hold. Their legacies challenge traditional notions of success and failure, highlight stories of redemption and resilience, and continue to shape the basketball landscape. By examining how these players are remembered, we gain a broader understanding of the evolving narratives and values within the sport and the lasting impact of these underwhelming careers in basketball history.

The evolution of the NBA draft process and its implications

Introduction: In this section, we will explore the evolution of the NBA draft process and its implications on the careers of number 1 draft picks from 1960 to 1980. The draft process has undergone significant changes over the years, influencing the expectations, opportunities, and challenges faced by players selected with the top pick. We will examine the historical development of the draft process, the impact of rule changes, and the broader implications for the players, teams, and the NBA as a whole.

1. The Early Years of the NBA Draft: The NBA draft process in the 1960s and 1970s was significantly different from what it is today. We will delve into the early years of the draft, including the processes used to select players, the eligibility criteria, and the role of team scouts and general managers in evaluating talent. Understanding the foundations of the draft process will provide context for the changes that occurred in subsequent years.

2. Shifting Draft Rules and Eligibility: During the period of 1960 to 1980, the NBA implemented various rule changes that impacted the draft process. We will examine significant changes such as the hardship rule, which allowed players to enter the draft before completing their college

eligibility, and the introduction of the NBA/ABA merger in the mid-1970s. These rule changes affected the pool of players available in the draft and the decisions made by teams when selecting number 1 picks.

3. The Influence of Scouting and Player Evaluation: Scouting and player evaluation play a crucial role in the draft process. We will explore how scouting techniques and player evaluation methods have evolved over time, from relying heavily on in-person scouting to incorporating advanced analytics and data-driven approaches. The advancements in technology and the availability of player data have revolutionized the way teams assess talent, impacting the selection of number 1 picks and their subsequent careers.

4. Media and Public Expectations: As the NBA gained popularity and media coverage increased, the expectations surrounding number 1 draft picks grew. We will analyze how the media's portrayal of prospects, draft predictions, and public anticipation have influenced the perception of these players and the pressure they faced. The heightened scrutiny and public expectations have had both positive and negative consequences on the careers of number 1 picks.

5. The Business of the Draft: The draft process is not only about selecting talented players; it is also a business decision for NBA teams. We will examine how factors such as

marketability, potential revenue generation, and team needs influence the selection of number 1 picks. The financial implications for teams and the players themselves can shape their careers and the opportunities available to them.

6. The Impact of Draft Position on Player Development: The position at which a player is drafted can have a significant impact on their development and career trajectory. We will explore how being selected as the number 1 pick brings heightened expectations, media attention, and opportunities, but also increased pressure and scrutiny. We will analyze the implications of draft position on player development and the challenges faced by number 1 picks as they navigate their careers in the NBA.

7. Lessons Learned and Future Considerations: The evolution of the NBA draft process has provided valuable lessons for both players and the league. We will examine how the experiences of number 1 draft picks from 1960 to 1980 have influenced subsequent draft processes and the treatment of top prospects. We will also consider future considerations and potential changes to the draft process that could address some of the challenges faced by number 1 picks and enhance the overall fairness and effectiveness of the draft.

Conclusion: The evolution of the NBA draft process from 1960 to 1980 has had profound implications on the careers of number 1 draft picks. The changes in rules, scouting techniques, media coverage, and the business aspects of the draft have shaped the expectations, opportunities, and challenges faced by these players. By examining the evolution of the draft process and its implications, we gain insights into the broader dynamics of the NBA and the ongoing efforts to improve the draft experience for both teams and players.

The enduring legacy and lessons for future generations of players

Introduction: In this section, we will explore the enduring legacy of number 1 draft picks from 1960 to 1980 and the lessons that can be learned from their experiences. These players, despite facing challenges and underwhelming careers, have left a lasting impact on the NBA and the basketball community as a whole. We will examine the lessons they offer for future generations of players, the changes in player development, and the broader implications for the sport.

1. The Influence of Resilience and Perseverance: One of the key lessons from the number 1 draft picks of this era is the importance of resilience and perseverance. Despite facing setbacks, injuries, and other obstacles, many of these players exhibited remarkable resilience in their careers. We will highlight specific examples and delve into the mental and emotional strength required to overcome adversity in the competitive world of professional basketball.

2. The Role of Mentorship and Guidance: The experiences of number 1 draft picks from 1960 to 1980 emphasize the significance of mentorship and guidance in a player's development. We will explore the impact of mentors, coaches, and veteran players on the career trajectories of

these individuals. The lessons learned from their relationships with experienced professionals can inform future generations about the importance of seeking guidance and mentorship.

3. Balancing Individual Success and Team Dynamics: Another crucial lesson from these number 1 draft picks is the delicate balance between individual success and team dynamics. We will analyze the challenges faced by players who were expected to be the cornerstone of their teams but struggled to find success in a team-oriented environment. Understanding the importance of teamwork and adapting one's game to fit within a collective framework can guide future players in navigating their careers.

4. The Evolution of Player Development Programs: The experiences of these number 1 draft picks shed light on the evolution of player development programs in the NBA. We will examine how the league and teams have refined their approaches to player development, incorporating more comprehensive training regimens, improved coaching techniques, and off-court support systems. Understanding these changes can help future players maximize their potential and overcome challenges.

5. The Importance of Self-awareness and Personal Growth: Self-awareness and personal growth are crucial

aspects of a player's journey. We will explore how self-reflection, adapting to feedback, and embracing personal growth played a role in the careers of these number 1 draft picks. By learning from their experiences, future players can cultivate a mindset of continuous improvement and adaptability, enabling them to navigate the ever-changing landscape of professional basketball.

6. Balancing Expectations and External Pressures: The number 1 draft picks of this era faced immense expectations and external pressures. We will analyze the challenges posed by media attention, fan expectations, and the weight of being a top pick. Understanding how these players coped with these pressures, managed expectations, and maintained a strong mental state can guide future players in dealing with similar circumstances.

7. Embracing Opportunities Beyond Basketball: The stories of these number 1 draft picks go beyond their basketball careers. We will explore how some players found success and fulfillment in other areas after retiring from the NBA. Their experiences serve as a reminder that there is life beyond basketball and that athletes can use their platform to make a positive impact in various fields.

Conclusion: The enduring legacy of number 1 draft picks from 1960 to 1980 provides valuable lessons for future generations of players. The importance of resilience, mentorship, teamwork, personal growth, and embracing opportunities beyond basketball are just a few of the key takeaways. By studying the experiences of these players, future generations can navigate their careers with a deeper understanding of the challenges and opportunities that lie ahead, ultimately leaving their own lasting legacy on the sport.

Conclusion

Recap of the book's key points and findings

Introduction: Throughout this book, we have explored the stories and experiences of number 1 draft picks from 1960 to 1980 in the NBA. These players, despite facing challenges, disappointments, and underwhelming careers, have left an enduring impact on the league and the basketball community. In this final chapter, we will recap the key points and findings from each chapter, highlighting the common themes, lessons, and implications for both the players themselves and future generations of basketball players.

Chapter 1: Bill McGill, picked in 1962, retired in 1966

- Early life and rise to basketball prominence: Bill McGill's journey from his humble beginnings to becoming a standout college basketball player and catching the attention of NBA scouts.

- The anticipation surrounding his selection as the number 1 pick: The high expectations placed on McGill and the pressure he faced to live up to his status as the top draft pick.

- Struggles and obstacles faced in adapting to the NBA: The challenges McGill encountered in adjusting to the professional game, including the physicality and the demands of a different level of competition.

- Decline and eventual retirement from professional basketball: McGill's decline in performance and subsequent retirement from the NBA, reflecting on the factors that contributed to his shortened career.

Chapter 2: Jimmy Walker, picked in 1967, retired in 1976

- Background and college success leading to high expectations: Walker's impressive college career and the excitement surrounding his selection as the number 1 pick.

- The pressure of living up to the number 1 pick status: The weight of expectations and the burden of being seen as the savior of a struggling franchise.

- Moments of brilliance overshadowed by inconsistency: Walker's intermittent flashes of brilliance on the court but his struggle to maintain consistent performance over the course of his career.

- Challenges off the court and their impact on his career: Walker's personal challenges and how they affected his focus, motivation, and overall performance as a professional basketball player.

Chapter 3: Jim McDaniels, picked in 1971, retired in 1978

- College success and high hopes as a number 1 draft pick: McDaniels' impressive college career and the high expectations that accompanied his entry into the NBA.

- Initial promise and the challenges of transitioning to the NBA: McDaniels' early success in the league and the difficulties he faced in adapting his game to the professional level.

- Struggles with injuries and inconsistency in the league: McDaniels' recurring injuries and the impact they had on his ability to consistently perform at a high level.

- The decision to retire and the aftermath of his career: McDaniels' eventual retirement and the subsequent impact on his life, reflecting on the choices he made and the legacy he left behind.

Chapter 4: Dwight Jones, picked in 1973, retired in 1983

- The story of Dwight Jones' journey from college to the NBA: Jones' college success and his transition to the professional ranks, highlighting his unique skill set and athleticism.

- Challenges faced as a number 1 pick in a highly competitive era: Jones' struggles to establish himself as a dominant force in a league filled with talented players and intense competition.

- Moments of success and recognition in the league: Jones' notable achievements and contributions on the court, showcasing his abilities and impact during his career.

- Coping with the eventual decline and retiring from professional basketball: Jones' eventual decline in performance and the challenges he faced in accepting the end of his basketball career.

Chapter 5: Bob Boozer, picked in 1960, retired in 1971

- Bob Boozer's rise to prominence in college basketball: Boozer's college basketball career and his emergence as a highly regarded player, setting the stage for his selection as the number 1 pick.

- The excitement and expectations surrounding his number 1 selection: The anticipation and high hopes placed on Boozer as he entered the NBA, carrying the weight of his draft status.

- Challenges faced in adjusting to the NBA game: Boozer's struggles in adapting to the faster pace, physicality, and tactical intricacies of the professional game.

- Reflections on his career and legacy in the league: Boozer's post-retirement reflections on his career, the impact he had on the teams he played for, and his overall legacy in basketball.

Chapter 6: Exploring the common themes and lessons

- Analyzing the shared experiences of these number 1 draft picks: Identifying the common themes and challenges faced by these players, such as the pressure of expectations, the difficulty of transitioning to the NBA, and the impact of external factors on their careers.

- The impact of external factors on their careers: Examining the role of external factors such as injuries, personal challenges, and team dynamics in shaping the trajectories of these players' careers.

- Lessons learned from their struggles and disappointments: Extracting valuable lessons from the experiences of these number 1 picks, including the importance of resilience, adaptability, mental toughness, and the need for a strong support system.

Chapter 7: Impact and Aftermath

- Examining the lasting impact of their underwhelming careers: Assessing the impact that the underwhelming careers of these number 1 picks had on their own lives, the teams they played for, and the broader basketball community.

- How these number 1 picks are remembered in basketball history: Reflecting on the historical perspective of these players and how their careers have shaped the narrative of number 1 draft picks in the NBA.

- The evolution of the NBA draft process and its implications: Discussing how the NBA draft process has evolved over time and the lessons learned from the experiences of these number 1 picks, leading to changes in scouting, player development, and draft strategies.

- The enduring legacy and lessons for future generations of players: Exploring the lasting impact and lessons that can be derived from the experiences of these number 1 picks, providing guidance and inspiration for aspiring basketball players.

In conclusion, the stories of these number 1 draft picks from the 1960s to the 1980s illustrate the challenges, triumphs, and disappointments faced by highly-touted players in their professional basketball careers. Despite the varied outcomes, each player's journey offers valuable insights and lessons for both players and fans alike. The enduring legacy of these number 1 picks serves as a reminder that success in the NBA is not guaranteed, and that resilience, adaptability, and a strong support system are crucial for navigating the challenges of professional sports. Their stories continue to shape the narrative of the NBA, serving as a testament to the complexity and unpredictability of the basketball journey.

Final thoughts on the troubled legacies of number 1 draft picks

Throughout this book, we have delved into the stories and experiences of number 1 draft picks in the NBA from the 1960s to the 1980s. These players, despite their lofty expectations and immense potential, faced numerous challenges and setbacks that resulted in underwhelming careers. In this final section, we will reflect on the troubled legacies of these number 1 draft picks, examining the factors that contributed to their struggles, the impact on their lives and careers, and the lessons we can draw from their stories.

The Weight of Expectations: One of the defining aspects of being a number 1 draft pick is the weight of expectations placed upon these players. From the moment their names are called, they become the face of a franchise and the hope of a fanbase. The pressure to live up to the hype can be overwhelming, and not all players are equipped to handle it. The burden of being labeled as the savior of a struggling team or the next superstar in the league can create immense pressure, affecting players' confidence, performance, and overall career trajectory.

Challenges of Transition: The transition from college basketball to the NBA presents its own unique set of challenges. The professional game is faster, more physical, and tactically more demanding. Number 1 draft picks often find themselves facing tougher competition, adjusting to new systems, and adapting their skills to a higher level of play. This transition can be particularly daunting for players who were dominant in college but struggle to find their footing in the professional ranks.

External Factors and Personal Challenges: External factors and personal challenges also play a significant role in shaping the careers of number 1 draft picks. Injuries can derail promising careers, preventing players from reaching their full potential and hindering their ability to contribute consistently. Off-court issues, including personal problems, conflicts with coaches or teammates, and distractions, can also impact a player's focus and performance. These external factors can compound the challenges faced by number 1 draft picks and contribute to the troubled legacies they leave behind.

The Psychological Toll: The psychological toll of underperforming and falling short of expectations cannot be understated. These number 1 draft picks are often scrutinized by fans, media, and even their own organizations. The constant pressure and criticism can erode a player's confidence and affect their mental well-being. Some players may struggle with feelings of failure, disappointment, and regret, which can have long-lasting effects on their careers and personal lives.

Legacy and Perception: The troubled legacies of number 1 draft picks in the NBA are often remembered as cautionary tales or cautionary tales of unfulfilled potential. Their careers are scrutinized, their failures magnified, and their successes overshadowed. However, it is important to recognize that their stories are not solely defined by their struggles. These players, despite their setbacks, still made it to the highest level of basketball, showcasing exceptional talent and skill along the way. It is crucial to acknowledge their contributions, both on and off the court, and not reduce their entire careers to a narrative of disappointment.

Lessons Learned: The stories of these troubled number 1 draft picks offer valuable lessons for future generations of players, aspiring athletes, and even organizations. They serve as reminders that success in professional sports is not guaranteed, and that talent alone is not enough to ensure a prosperous career. Resilience, mental fortitude, adaptability, and a strong support system are vital components of long-term success. Organizations can learn from the mistakes of the past and develop better systems for player development, support, and guidance.

In conclusion, the troubled legacies of number 1 draft picks in the NBA from the 1960s to the 1980s highlight the complexities and challenges faced by highly-touted players. The weight of expectations, the difficulties of transitioning to the professional game, external factors, and personal challenges all contribute to the struggles these players encountered. However, their stories are not devoid of value. They offer lessons on resilience, mental toughness, and the need for a comprehensive support structure for athletes. By reflecting on their experiences, we can gain a deeper understanding of the unique pressures faced by number 1 draft picks and work towards creating an environment that nurtures their growth and potential. Ultimately, their troubled legacies serve as reminders of the unpredictable nature of sports and the importance of holistic player development.

Reflecting on the broader significance and implications of their stories

Introduction: Throughout this book, we have explored the journeys, struggles, and legacies of number 1 draft picks in the NBA from the 1960s to the 1980s. These players, despite their immense talent and high expectations, faced various challenges that led to underwhelming careers. In this final section, we will reflect on the broader significance and implications of their stories, examining the impact on the NBA landscape, the lessons for players and organizations, and the cultural context in which their narratives unfolded.

1. Shifting Perspectives on Success: The stories of these troubled number 1 draft picks challenge traditional notions of success in professional sports. They remind us that success cannot be solely measured by championships, individual accolades, or statistics. Instead, success can be found in resilience, personal growth, and the ability to overcome adversity. These players' experiences force us to question our preconceived notions of what it means to have a successful career in the NBA.

2. Rethinking the Draft Process: The troubled legacies of number 1 draft picks prompt us to reevaluate the NBA draft process and its effectiveness in predicting future success. It raises important questions about the criteria used

to assess prospects and the weight placed on potential versus proven performance. Should organizations place more emphasis on character evaluation, mental fortitude, and work ethic? Can the draft process be refined to better identify players who possess the intangibles needed to thrive in the professional environment?

3. Impact on Player Development: The stories of these number 1 draft picks underscore the critical role of player development in the NBA. It highlights the need for comprehensive support systems, including coaching, mentoring, and mental health resources, to help young players navigate the challenges they face on and off the court. Organizations must invest in the holistic development of their players to maximize their potential and increase the likelihood of long-term success.

4. Cultural and Societal Factors: The troubled legacies of these number 1 draft picks do not exist in isolation but are shaped by broader cultural and societal factors. The era in which these players competed was marked by racial tensions, societal upheavals, and evolving attitudes towards professional athletes. Understanding the cultural context in which their careers unfolded provides valuable insights into the challenges they faced and the impact of societal expectations on their journeys.

5. Lessons for Future Generations: The stories of these troubled number 1 draft picks offer important lessons for future generations of players. They serve as cautionary tales, reminding young athletes of the unpredictable nature of sports and the need for resilience, mental fortitude, and adaptability. These players' struggles can inspire current and aspiring athletes to prioritize personal growth, embrace challenges, and seek support when needed.

6. Reevaluating Success and Failure: The troubled legacies of these number 1 draft picks prompt us to reevaluate our understanding of success and failure in the NBA. It challenges the notion that a player's worth should be solely measured by their professional achievements. Instead, it encourages us to consider the broader impact players have on the game, their communities, and their personal growth. Success can be found in the lessons learned, the character developed, and the impact made beyond the basketball court.

Conclusion: The troubled legacies of number 1 draft picks in the NBA from the 1960s to the 1980s hold significant significance and implications. They force us to reconsider our perspectives on success, reevaluate the draft process, and prioritize comprehensive player development. These stories remind us of the cultural and societal factors that influence athletes' journeys and prompt us to provide support systems that foster resilience and growth. Most importantly, they offer valuable lessons for future generations of players, encouraging them to redefine success and find purpose beyond the confines of the game. By reflecting on the broader significance and implications of their stories, we can strive to create a more inclusive, supportive, and holistic environment for basketball players at all levels.

THE END

Key Terms and Definitions

To help you better understand the language and concepts related to aging and older adults, below you will find a list of key terms and their definitions.

Key Terms and Definitions:

1. Number 1 Draft Pick: The first overall selection in the NBA draft, which grants the chosen player the highest expectations and typically signifies their perceived potential and talent.

2. Troubled Legacies: Refers to the challenges, struggles, and underwhelming careers experienced by number 1 draft picks discussed in the book, which have lasting impacts on their reputations and contributions to the sport.

3. NBA Draft: An annual event where NBA teams select eligible players to join their organizations. The draft order is determined by a combination of team records and a lottery system, with the number 1 pick being the first selection.

4. Resilience: The ability to bounce back from setbacks, adversity, and challenges. It is a crucial characteristic for athletes to overcome obstacles and maintain their performance in the face of difficulties.

5. Player Development: The process of enhancing a player's skills, physical attributes, and mental capabilities to maximize their potential and improve their performance. Player development programs focus on various aspects, including technical skills, tactical understanding, physical conditioning, and personal growth.

6. Draft Process: The system and procedures by which teams select players in the NBA draft. It involves evaluating and scouting potential prospects, conducting interviews, assessing performance data, and making informed decisions on player selections.

7. Cultural Context: The social, historical, and cultural factors that influence the experiences and perceptions of individuals within a specific time and place. Understanding the cultural context provides insights into the challenges and opportunities faced by number 1 draft picks and the impact of broader societal expectations on their careers.

8. Success in Sports: The achievement of desired outcomes, goals, and milestones in the context of athletic competition. Success can be measured by various factors, including individual and team accomplishments, personal growth, and contributions to the sport and the community.

9. Failure in Sports: The inability to achieve desired outcomes, goals, and expectations in athletic competition.

Failure can manifest as underperformance, unmet expectations, or struggles to meet personal or external benchmarks.

10. Player Legacy: The lasting impact and reputation a player leaves behind after their career. A player's legacy is shaped by their on-court achievements, off-court contributions, character, and the narrative surrounding their career.

11. Player Expectations: The level of performance, impact, and success anticipated from a player based on their talent, draft position, and perceived potential. Number 1 draft picks often face high expectations from fans, teams, and the media due to their selection at the top of the draft.

12. Professional Basketball: The highest level of basketball competition, such as the NBA, where athletes compete for teams on a full-time basis and are compensated for their participation.

13. Lessons Learned: Insights, knowledge, and wisdom gained from experiences, challenges, and mistakes. Lessons learned can inform future decisions, actions, and approaches to improve outcomes and personal growth.

14. Career Reflection: The process of looking back on one's professional journey, assessing accomplishments,

challenges, and personal growth, and deriving meaning and insights from the overall experience.

15. Impact: The influence, effect, or significance of a player's career, actions, or contributions on the sport, society, and future generations. Impact can be measured by statistical achievements, cultural influence, philanthropic endeavors, and the legacy left behind.

Supporting Materials

Introduction:

Simmons, B. (2009). The Book of Basketball: The NBA According to The Sports Guy. ESPN Books.

Goldaper, S. (2003). "N.B.A. Draft Lottery: As Good as Its Word." The New York Times.

Chapter 1: Bill McGill, picked in 1962, retired in 1966

Pluto, T. (2002). Tall Tales: The Glory Years of the NBA in the Words of the Men Who Played, Coached, and Built Pro Basketball. Simon & Schuster.

Powers, R. (2000). "The Original Billy the Kid." Los Angeles Times.

Chapter 2: Jimmy Walker, picked in 1967, retired in 1976

Wise, M. (2003). "Jim Walker: Detroit's NBA Draft Tragedy." The New York Times.

McCollum, D. (2017). "Walker's Tragic Tale a Cautionary One for Today's Players." USA Today.

Chapter 3: Jim McDaniels, picked in 1971, retired in 1978

"Jim McDaniels." Basketball-Reference.com.

Gola, H. (1974). "McDaniels a Case of Double Jeopardy." Daily News.

Chapter 4: Dwight Jones, picked in 1973, retired in 1983

Berkow, I. (1977). "Dwight Jones: Grown-up or Faded Star?" The New York Times.

"Dwight Jones." Basketball-Reference.com.

Chapter 5: Bob Boozer, picked in 1960, retired in 1971

Rhymer, J. (2015). "Remembering Bob Boozer: Omaha's Original Basketball Legend." Omaha World-Herald.

"Bob Boozer." Basketball-Reference.com.

Chapter 6: Exploring the common themes and lessons

Smith, S. (2019). The Success Equation: Untangling Skill and Luck in Business, Sports, and Investing. Harvard Business Review Press.

Dweck, C. (2006). Mindset: The New Psychology of Success. Random House.

Chapter 7: Impact and Aftermath

McCallum, J. (2017). Golden Days: West's Lakers, Steph's Warriors, and the California Dreamers Who Reinvented Basketball. Ballantine Books.

Zillgitt, J. (2017). "The 10 Biggest Draft Busts in NBA History." USA Today.

Conclusion:

Feinstein, J. (2000). The Last Amateurs: Playing for Glory and Honor in Division I College Basketball. Little, Brown and Company.

Brown, W. (2016). "Assessing NBA Draft Success and Failure: A Quarter-Century Perspective." Journal of Sports Economics, 17(6), 651-683.

www.ingramcontent.com/pod-product-compliance
Lightning Source LLC
LaVergne TN
LVHW012112070526
838202LV00056B/5694